Modern Stoves For All

Revised Edition

by Waclaw Micuta

illustrated by Hugo Kehrli

Practical ACTION PUBLISHING

Intermediate Technology Publications
in association with **The Bellerive Foundation 1985**

Practical Action Publishing Ltd
27a Albert Street, Rugby, CV21 2SG, Warwickshire, UK
www.practicalactionpublishing.org

© Intermediate Technology Publications 1986

First published 1985 \Digitised 2013
Reprinted in the UK, 2020
Reprinted by Practical Action Publishing
Rugby, Warwickshire UK

ISBN 10: 0 94668 835 4
ISBN 13: 9780946688357
ISBN Library Ebook: 9781780442860
Book DOI: http://dx.doi.org/10.3362/9781780442860

A catalogue record for this book is available from the British Library.

Since 1974, Practical Action Publishing has published and disseminated books and
information in support of international development work throughout the world.
Practical Action Publishing is a trading name of Practical Action Publishing Ltd
(Company Reg. No. 1159018), the wholly owned publishing company of Practical Action.
Practical Action Publishing trades only in support of its parent charity objectives and any
profits are covenanted back to Practical Action (Charity Reg. No. 247257, Group VAT
Registration No. 880 9924 76).

CONTENTS

Figures

Tables

Foreword
by Prince Sadruddin Aga Khan

In the face of man's relentless and indiscriminate plundering of nature, more and more people are beginning fully to appreciate the vulnerability of our planet's life support systems. Indeed, conservationists warn that unless urgent action is taken in the very near future, our children will inherit a barren, polluted and decimated world.

We must stop indulging in abstract debate on the ecological problems threatening our very survival and take **concrete** steps to reverse trends that are already assuming disaster proportions.

A good example of what may be achieved is the pioneering work of Waclaw Micuta in the promotion of more rational means of utilising primary and renewable energy so as to alleviate the unduly heavy burden being placed on the earth's rapidly receding forest reserves.

This second edition of *Modern Stoves for All* provides clear evidence of the contribution that may be made, by individuals as well as by non-governmental and small private organisations. More significantly, it illustrates that work of lasting value may be undertaken with relatively modest means.

On the basis of the field tests already conducted, I am confident that the fuel-saving stoves, bread ovens and heating devices described in this booklet will not share the fate of many other models destined for developing countries. In the past, many such stoves have, despite the vast sums invested, failed to win the acceptance of rural populations simply because they have not performed well enough to induce a changeover from wasteful traditional methods such as open-fire cooking.

One of the attractions of the Micuta stoves lies in the fact that they form the focal point of a comprehensive package deal of measures which notably emphasise the use of alternative fuels such as waste briquettes, biogas, natural gas, kerosene, diesel oil, peat or coal. Great importance is also attached to the manufacture of standardised cooking pots, the supply of essential metal components, the promotion of more rational cooking methods and the introduction of simple fuel-saving devices such as hay boxes.

The cooking and baking systems proposed sometimes call for additional expenditure. However, national authorities and international organisations must realise that some expense is bound to be involved in the development and manufacture of truly efficient stoves capable of making an impact on long-term energy saving, and consequently the economic interests of developing countries. The poor cannot be expected to bear the entire burden themselves. Some form of assistance is therefore essential and should be regarded as an investment for future prosperity.

In view of the pressing need for action, it is my sincere hope that this booklet will receive a favourable hearing from those — particularly governments and inter-governmental organisations — with the resources to support the various measures proposed.

Introduction

It is generally agreed that one of the principal causes of the rapid deforestation that is occurring in many developing countries has been the excessive use of firewood and charcoal for cooking and baking purposes. It is also generally agreed that the large-scale introduction of efficient fuel-saving stoves, bread ovens and improved cooking methods, coupled with increasing efforts to plant more trees, could go a long way towards reversing these disastrous trends and help to restore the balance between the growing and consumption of firewood.

Despite this general consensus, however, progress has been disappointingly slow and attempts to introduce efficient stoves have met so far with only limited success.

By way of contrast, many far less essential commodities, such as motorcyles, sewing machines or transistor radios, are being accepted without difficulty by local populations.

Perhaps the principal reason for this paradox is that the above-mentioned products generally render **good service** whilst many of the stoves proposed to date do not.

In addition, behind transistor radios, motorcycles and the like there are professionals who have the training and experience to promote them and ensure maintenance and repairs. If responsibility for introducing stoves could be similarly entrusted to qualified technicians and experts in promotion there is no reason why fuel-efficient stoves should not gain widespread acceptance in the same way as sewing machines — provided, of course, that their cost is compatible with the available purchasing power. In this latter context, appropriate action on the part of governments, together with assistance from bi-lateral and multi-lateral sources, is of the utmost importance. Without such action it will not be possible to stop — and ultimately reverse — the ecological disasters threatening several regions of the world today.

This booklet is not addressed to **individuals** who wish to build stoves as the author does not believe that really efficient stoves can be constructed by inexperienced amateurs. It was not the case in the past, and it is not the case today. On the contrary, stove building has always been a profession and an art. It must, consequently, be carried out by properly trained craftsmen and craftswomen. Where necessary, they should be supplied with essential components, such as heating plates, grates, metal sheet chimneys and cowls, as well as brushes for sweeping chimneys, moulds and cooking pots.

Modern Stoves for All is thus addressed to skilled technicians, in the hope that they will use the general drawings provided as a basis for building stove models, which they will then test and adapt to local conditions.

Even technicians are warned that their first attempts will rarely prove satisfactory for, whilst the concept of the stoves presented herein is relatively simple, a certain amount of practice and experience is required to master their construction and use.

Our aim is not to supply ready-made answers to the complex problems facing stove designers, but rather to set out ideas and suggestions for further consideration and trials. The stoves were selected, from among many different models, on the basis of good service rendered during field tests in Europe, Africa, Asia and the Caribbean.

The main intention of this publication is to show what it is possible to achieve in the immediate future without waiting for "wonder stoves" that may never leave the drawing boards of equipment designers.

This latest English edition differs significantly from the first one, published in 1981 under the auspices of the Bellerive Foundation in Geneva. Several stove models have been removed, specifications of others modified and new models added. These changes reflect further field experience and, in particular, continuous testing of the fuel efficiency of the models concerned.

The new stove models and design improvements described in this edition are mainly due to the advice and assistance of Mr Emil Haas, a retired Swiss industrialist and specialist on heating installations, who has graciously offered, for the benefit of the poor, his craftsmanship and lifelong experience. This publication could not have been revised without his dedication, inventiveness and enthusiasm, for which I am most grateful and indebted. I am also indebted to Barry Gilbert-Miguet who edited and prepared the text for publication.

Waclaw Micuta
Geneva
January 1985.

PART ONE

BASIC
PRINCIPLES

A. Firewood as a fuel

Firewood was one of the first fuels to be used for cooking and heating purposes, since it was readily available and relatively easy to ignite. Even today about half of humanity, living for the most part in developing countries, depends on wood for survival. Excessive use has, however, resulted in a serious depletion of the earth's forest reserves which, besides causing considerable human suffering, has led to soil erosion on a massive scale, the silting of water reservoirs and the rapid expansion of arid and desert areas.

If we are to curb these catastrophic trends before it is too late it is vital to promote a more rational utilisation of primary and renewable energy geared to the specific needs of the people. The scope for wood saving is immense when it is considered that, in many parts of the world, up to 90% of all the wood cut is used solely for cooking and heating purposes.

Prior to the industrial revolution, problems similar to those currently facing rural populations throughout the Third World were encountered by our ancestors in Asia, Europe and North America. Their experience, gained over centuries, reveals a wealth of human ingenuity in the efficient use of wood that may be usefully applied to meeting the needs of the poor in developing countries.

Naturally, the progress made by science in determining the best methods of extracting thermal energy from various fuels should not be overlooked. Where appropriate, traditional implements may be adapted or improved in the light of modern technology.

Ultimately, it should be possible to produce designs for stoves that are simple, highly efficient, and capable of being manufactured by village craftsmen using — with the addition of some metal components coming from outside — materials that are available locally. The cost of such stoves should be low but they must, nonetheless, be of good quality and give satisfactory results. Governments may assist in this respect by means of appropriate economic measures which will not only ensure that rural communities enjoy efficient, low-cost cooking facilities, but also secure the protection of forests.

B. The essentials of efficient stoves

If fuel saving is to be achieved there are two essential principles that must be incorporated into any stove design. The first is the complete combustion of the fuel. A simple means of judging the efficiency of a stove is to observe the colour of the smoke it gives off. If this is darkish it means that part of the fuel is not being consumed and is escaping in the form of unburnt particles. A more detailed analysis of the smoke leaving a stove may be carried out with the aid of Orsat measuring equipment.

The second basic requirement of an efficient stove is that the maximum use should be made of the heat generated for the purpose intended. As far as cooking is concerned, the efficiency of a stove is measured by comparing the total volume of heat generated in the fire-box with that absorbed by the contents of the pot. This measurement is discussed briefly towards the end of this booklet.

C. The main characteristics of firewood

Composition

In order to extract maximum heat it is important to understand the particular

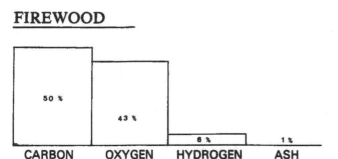

FIREWOOD

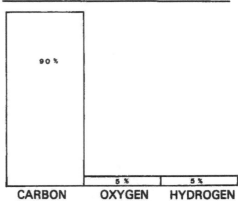

HARD COAL

characteristics of firewood that distinguish it, especially as far as combustion is concerned, from other fuels with organic origins such as peat, lignite, hard coal or crude oil (see Figure 1).

The thermal value of firewood lies in the high proportion of combustible gases, which should be completely burnt in the stove rather than allowed to escape with the smoke. Indeed, it may be said that it is not so much wood that burns as the gases it releases! Due to its high oxygen content, firewood requires less air for combustion than most other fuels, and careful regulation of air input is thus important if turbulent, and consequently inefficient, burning is to be avoided.

Heat value

The heat value of a fuel is usually defined as the quantity of heat extracted from 1 kg of matter when it is burnt. It is usually expressed in kilo calories (kcal/kg) or kilo joules (kJ). The heat value of any given variety of wood depends on its density and water content. For example, well-seasoned hardwood with 15 to 17% moisture content has a heat value of about 3,700 kcal/kg or 15,500 kJ/kg. This figure is approximately halved with wood waste in the form of bundles or faggots.

Density

In Europe, hornbeam, beech, ash and oak, which all have high densities, are considered to be among the best varieties for firewood purposes, while soft and resinous species such as pine and spruce, with lower densities, are preferred for kindling. Unfortunately, in developing countries such a wide choice is not always available, and people have to make do with whatever species are available locally. This fact should be borne in mind by those responsible for tree planting programmes, who sometimes tend to place too much emphasis on resistance to climate and rate of growth and overlook the importance of the heat value of the trees planted.

Moisture content

Besides increasing the danger of chimney fire,[1] an unduly high moisture content — about 20% and above — slows the combustion process, lowers the temperature in the fire-box and generally renders it difficult for volatile particles to burn completely

As can be seen from the following table, it is a waste of energy to burn newly cut firewood without first reducing the moisture content through some form of drying procedure:[2]

1. By causing deposits of creosote and tar in the chimney.
2. In Europe, newly cut firewood contains about 50% moisture. Chopped, covered and dried in the open air for about two years, it still contains 15 to 17% moisture. To burn firewood containing a greater percentage of moisture is a waste of energy.

	kcal/kg	kJ/kg
Newly cut wood	1,950	8,200
Wood well dried in open air	3,700	15,500
Wood dried in oven	4,500	18,800

Simple measures, like stacking some wood close to the stove, may further reduce moisture content and thereby increase the heat value of firewood.

D. The process of wood combustion

Basically, firewood contains two combustible substances: carbon and hydrogen. Combustion takes place when the wood is heated, causing these substances and their derivatives to escape in the form of gases and mix with oxygen from the air. This complex process is accompanied by a strong generation of heat, and a flame is produced when the wood reaches a temperature of about 250°C.

Optimal size of firewood

Wood is a good insulator, which means that heat tends to penetrate it very slowly. Thus, the thicker the wood, the longer it will take for its inner layers to gasify and generate heat. For this reason, when cooking it is recommended to use wood with a small diameter, if possible not surpassing 3 to 4 cm. Small pieces of wood release gases easily and give off a steady flame.

Air supply

To ensure proper combustion it is necessary to provide an adequate, but not excessive, supply of air. In practice, not all the air entering a stove is used in the chemical process of combustion. Some of it simply passes through and it is thus necessary to admit more air (known as excess air) than is theoretically needed. Usually, for the correct functioning of a stove the ratio of excess air[4] should be between 1.5 and 2.0. This being said, however, it is important to regulate the flow of air according to the requirements of each stage of combustion.[5]

E. The stages of wood combustion

For a better understanding, the process of wood combustion may be divided into three stages:

Stage 1

Moisture in the wood begins to evaporate and the temperature rises to about 100°C. The higher the moisture content of the wood, the more this initial stage is prolonged with consequent loss of energy.

Stage 2

As the temperature rises, the second stage begins with decomposition of the wood. At a temperature of about 150°C, the release of gases begins and semi-liquid tar starts to appear. The wood smoulders and gives off dark smoke and a strong smell. This stage should be avoided by maintaining a steady flame from the outset of combustion as the smoke indicates that valuable particles are being lost. In addition, greasy tar accumulates in the stove and chimney and creates a danger of chimney fire.

3. Source: *Chauffage Moderne au Bois*, L'Office Forestier Central Suisse, CH-4500 Soleure.
4. Calculated by placing the volume of all air actually admitted to the stove over that theoretically required for combustion.
5. At first a liberal amount of air should be supplied. At the peak of combustion and later, towards its completion, the flow of air should be gradually reduced.

Stage 3

The third stage, termed 'full combustion', commences at around 225°C and reaches a peak at about 300°C. Above this temperature the wood is gradually transformed into glowing embers. Between 260° and 290°C there is a tendency for combustion to become over turbulent. If this occurs it should be slowed down by reducing the air supply, the draught or both. Figure 3 summarises the various stages of combustion in graph form.

Figure 3 *The stages of wood combustion.*

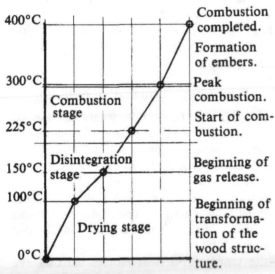

Source: Op. cit. *Chauffage Moderne au Bois*, p.4.

Flame temperature

The temperature of the flame given off during combustion may easily exceed 800°C. Naturally, if a pot is surrounded by flames, such intense heat will cause food to boil rapidly and result in efficient use of the wood burned. If, however, the flames touch only part of the pot's surface, the effect of heat absorption is considerably diminished. This partly explains the popularity of open-fire cooking in developing countries and why, in Europe and North America, cooking pots were always lowered into the fire-boxes of wood-burning stoves to ensure direct contact with the flames and thus economise on fuel.

Fire-lighters

The art of making a good fire lies in producing flames at the very beginning of combustion. This may easily be achieved by using chips, small twigs or faggots of particularly dry and inflammable wood. A good fire-lighter is a piece of dry, resinous,[6] round-shaped wood of about 5 cm in diameter and splintered at one end in the form of a brush. This begins by burning like a torch but then settles down to produce a steady flame. Bellows are also very useful and should form part of standard stove equipment. Where they are not available, a long metal pipe, fluted at one end so as to enable air to be blown into the fire, may be used instead.

F. Primary and secondary air

The importance of secondary air

As has been seen, it is necessary to provide stoves with air in order to ensure proper combustion. When this air is supplied from below the grate it is known as **primary** air. If only primary air is supplied, as is often the case with small wood stoves, there is a danger of inefficient use of fuel in that there may not be enough air in the upper part of the fire-box to burn all the combustible gases released from the wood. To avoid losing these valuable gases, modern stoves — irrespective of size — often provide for a supply of **secondary** air in the upper part of the fire-box.

In the interests of fuel economy the models featured in this book adopt this important innovation and provide for a supply of pre-heated secondary air.

Pre-heating the air supply

As mentioned above, combustion requires

---

6. In Europe, fires are often started with dry coniferous wood which rapidly develops good flames and facilitates the burning of other varieties of wood.

a temperature of approximately 250 to 300°C. It follows that if the air supplied for combustion is not pre-heated in some way before it flows into the fire-box it may do more harm than good by **cooling** the gases and preventing them from burning. In practice, the problem only arises with the secondary air supply since primary air, which comes from below, is well heated as it passes through the hot, glowing embers that accumulate on the grate during combustion. Providing for the efficient pre-heating of secondary air is a more complex matter which requires more thought. The problem is somewhat easier to resolve in metal stoves than in clay or brick models, due to the greater heat conductivity of metals.

G. Winning acceptance for new methods

Despite considerable efforts to introduce improved stoves, cooking by open fire continues to be the most popular method in developing countries.

In many instances the underlying reason for this preference is not so much attachment to tradition, or reluctance to accept change, but rather, quite simply, that many of the suggested stoves have failed to give satisfactory service. Because of this, womenfolk have tended to reject the new innovations and continue with traditional methods which, for them, present distinct advantages that must be clearly understood by stove designers if more acceptable alternatives are to be developed.

Advantages of open-fire cooking

—no expense is involved for the rural poor.
—the only implements needed are three stones on which to stand the pots.
—the cooking pot may be placed directly in the flames. If the fire is well managed and protected from wind, fuel efficiency is quite good.
—by removing some of the wood from under the pot it is simple to regulate the heat and allow for simmering.
—the 'three stones' system is flexible and can cater for any size of pot.
—it is easy to use several pots over one fire, which is important for family cooking.
—no maintenance or repair is necessary.
—the firewood need not be cut into small pieces before use.[7]
—after use, the fire may be easily extinguished with sand or earth and the unburnt branches kept for future use.

These advantages of open-fire cooking should be contrasted with the obvious disadvantages:

Disadvantages of open-fire cooking

—it often represents a wasteful use of firewood and is, thus, a major cause of deforestation in developing countries.
—open-fires are difficult to use in rain or wind.
—the cooking pots are not stable; the user must hold them in place with one hand whilst stirring the contents with the other.
—the smoke and heat causes serious eye and respiratory complaints. To cook over an open fire represents a real hardship to women.
—there is a risk that the fire may get out of control and spread.
—there is a danger of accidents, particularly to children.
—it is difficult to maintain a steady flame.

Thus, if we are to popularise new cooking methods among women in developing countries, it is essential that the alternatives proposed should not only eliminate the disadvantages of open fire cooking, but also retain the **advantages**. In particular, it is important that new models should have a higher fuel-efficiency rate than the well-

7. The fact that the rural poor usually have no saws, wedges or good axes is often overlooked.

6

managed open fire discussed on pages 29 to 31. To date, this has rarely been the case.[8]

In the past, these considerations have tended to be overlooked and many of the new stoves proposed have proved to be of limited practical use in the field and have, consequently, failed to win the acceptance of rural populations.

In this context, we can learn much from the experience of our ancestors in Asia, Europe and North America who, by **gradual evolution**, have already provided solutions to most of the problems involved in the changeover from open-fire cooking to more efficient methods. Much of this basic and **proven** knowledge may be usefully revised and applied to the manufacture of stoves for developing countries.

Let us then briefly examine the steps that led to the abandonment of open-fire cooking in **developed** countries.

H. The evolution from open fires to modern stoves in developed countries

There are three basic factors which contribute to wastage of heat (and consequently energy) if cooking is carried out on an open fire, using poorly designed utensils. The technical terms used to describe each of these factors (together with their meanings in the present context) are as follows:
—**radiation**, which means loss of heat to the environment.
—**convection**, which means loss of heat caused by the upward movement of gases.
—**conduction**, which describes the movement of heat through solid materials.

The evolution from open-fire cooking in developed countries depended on a long, empirical study of each of these phenomena.

Diminishing heat loss through radiation

When an open fire is used it is not always possible to direct **all** the heat generated onto the pot itself. A large proportion will obviously tend to escape from the **sides** of the fire into the environment. To prevent such loss, and thus make the maximum use of the heat generated for the purpose intended (i.e. to heat the pot), the logical solution was to enclose the fire in some way. For this purpose, it was necessary to employ materials that were good insulators, and our ancestors first used stones, then clay and later bricks. Nowadays there is a tendency to use somewhat more sophisticated insulating materials for the stoves used in developed countries, but it should be remembered that these are expensive and that **they do not appreciably increase the efficiency of the stoves**. The more traditional materials, such as clay, thus remain eminently suitable for use in countries where they are readily available.

Reducing heat loss caused by convection

Heat also tends to escape from **above** the stove because hot air or gases rise and are replaced with cold air coming from outside. This problem was alleviated by enclosing the top of the stove and allowing the hot air to flow by means of ducts and chimneys. In addition, the cooking pots were carefully positioned so that as much as possible of the available heat could be absorbed by them.

8. A well-managed open fire in **field** conditions will give a rate of about 20%. Much higher percentages may be achieved under laboratory conditions, as has been shown by the research into open fires conducted by Eindhoven University (see discussion on well-managed open fires, page 29).

Increasing heat absorption by conduction

As has been seen, considerable efforts were made to prevent heat from escaping and to retain it for as long as possible in the vicinity of the cooking pot. Ultimately, however, the object of cooking is not to heat the pot itself but rather its **contents**. Thus, our ancestors were quick to realise the importance of manufacturing pots out of materials with high conductivity — such as cast-iron, copper, and, later, aluminium or steel — instead of earthenware.

A more detailed study of the evolution outlined above reveals a wealth of knowledge and experience upon which we may usefully draw when designing stoves for developing countries — especially those where the shortage of firewood is most acute.

However, if modern cooking methods are to gain acceptance, two criteria are of fundamental importance. Firstly, as has been stated earlier, the proposed alternatives to open-fire cooking must give **satisfactory results** and, secondly, they must be **within the means of the poor rural communities for which they are intended**.

Thus, the promotion of efficient stoves requires not only patient effort on the part of technicians but also, and most importantly, **the political and financial support of governments concerned in the long-term energy saving and economic interests of their respective countries**.

I. Basic components of wood-burning stoves

The fire-box

The fire-box serves as a combustion chamber and must therefore be constructed of materials capable of withstanding high temperatures. In good stoves, it is equipped with air intake as well as air-with-gas mixing arrangements, and is designed so as to direct heat towards the cooking pot. For optimal efficiency, the fire-box should be in the form of an **inverted cone**, with the base considerably smaller than the top. This shape, besides allowing the pieces of fuel-wood to fall automatically into position as required, provides ample space for the released gases — and effectively limits the size of the grate which, in wood-burning stoves, should be fairly small for optimum performance.

Figure 4 presents two cross-sections of a modern fire-box supplied with both primary and secondary air.

The size of the fire-box will, obviously, depend to a large extent on the use to which the stove is to be put. If it is intended (as recommended in this book) to use cooking pots which are lowered into the fire-box, the internal height should be somewhat greater and space should be left around the pots to allow for the release and combustion of gases.

The grate

A properly designed grate will improve the efficiency of a stove, **as it allows for the recovery of the energy contained in both the flames and glowing embers**. In wood burning models it should be relatively small in size, and its surface must always be less than that of the bottom of the fire-box. During combustion the grate should be completely covered with glowing embers so as to maintain a high temperature in the fire-box and facilitate the combustion of gases by pre-heating the primary air supply. If the open surface of the grate is too large, it will cause excessive burning and wood consumption. On the other hand, if it is too small it will result in defective combustion.

Wood-burning stoves require far less air input than coal, coke or peat-burning models and, consequently, the open spaces

Figure 4 *Two cross-sections of a modern fire-box supplied with both primary and secondary air.*

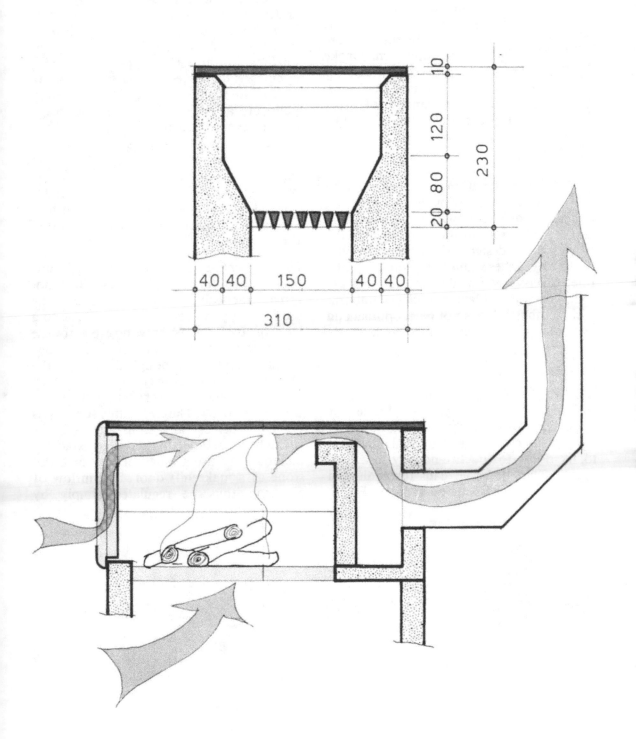

should represent no more than 30% of the total surface of the grate.

Experience has shown that cast-iron is the best material for manufacturing grates but, as an interim measure, until this is more widely available, local tinsmiths may make perfectly adequate substitutes out of construction or scrap iron (see designs of stoves). The main disadvantage of using these materials is that the grates will not be quite so durable as their cast-iron equivalents.

Ashes. An examination of the ashes left in the stove after use provides an excellent indication of the quality of combustion and, by extension, of the correctness of the stove's basic design proportions. Ideally, the leftover ashes should be in the form of a fine, silver-white powder. If the ashes are found to contain black particles of unburnt fuel, combustion has not been optimal and steps should be taken to improve it.

The doors

Ideally, combustion should take place within a closed fire-box — hence the importance of properly designed doors. In industrialised countries the usual practice is to fix doors to the fire-box by means of hinges. This, however, calls for additional expenditure which may be avoided. Figure

5 shows an alternative solution using doors made from scrap metal, which may be produced without difficulty by local craftsmen, and which are designed to fit **into** the stove opening. The inflow of primary air is regulated by means of an opening in the **ash-box door**. A similar opening is employed on the **fire-box door** to regulate the flow of secondary air. Here, however, a simple, inexpensive device is used to ensure that the air is correctly pre-heated.[9] A small metal box is welded or riveted to the fire-box door in such a way that it is in contact with the fire. The air passes through the regulated opening in the door, is heated as it flows through this box, and is finally ejected into the upper part of the fire-box.

Using unchopped firewood. In some regions the doors described above may not prove practicable, as they necessitate the use of **chopped** firewood. Where, due to a lack of tools, it is only possible to use **unchopped** wood, a specially small stove opening should be designed so that **the branches themselves** may be used to block the passage and thereby reduce and control the incoming air. Naturally, this solution is far from perfect and should be avoided whenever possible. A more satisfactory method is to use a block of clay or a flat stone as a makeshift door. The inflow of air may thus be regulated simply by

Figure 5 *Sheet-metal stove doors.*

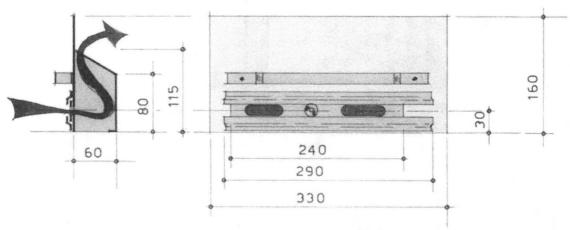

9. See p.5 on the importance and difficulty of pre-heating secondary air.

10

pushing the block in and out of the stove opening or by pushing the stone aside (see for example the design of the Community stove).

The heating plates

One of the principal reasons for the failure of certain stove models to win widespread acceptance and establish themselves in developing countries as satisfactory alternatives to cooking by open-fire has been the fact that they have not been equipped with **efficient covers in the form of heating plates.**

Indeed, the manufacture of these elements is one of the most critical factors in the design of an efficient stove — as was proved by the experience of our ancestors in developed countries.

The problem was in fact the object of much research in Europe during the last century and was successfully resolved with the massive, industrial production of standardised cast-iron heating plates equipped with rings to fit different sizes of pot (see Figure 6). This development constituted the **ultimate stage** in the evolution from open-fire to efficient cooking methods in developed countries. Most of the innovations that followed contributed little to improved efficiency.

Pending the local and widespread availability of cast-iron plates in developing countries, metal sheet (of 1.5 mm grade or 18 gauge) may be used to advantage by village craftsmen as a less durable but satisfactory alternative. A better solution would be to manufacture such plates in properly equipped workshops with thicker sheets — 2.0 mm or 16 gauge — and supply these to stove makers.

It cannot be stressed enough that in the design and construction of truly efficient wood stoves there is no satisfactory alternative to the use of cast-iron or sheet metal heating plates.

Figure 6 *Cast-iron heating plate.*

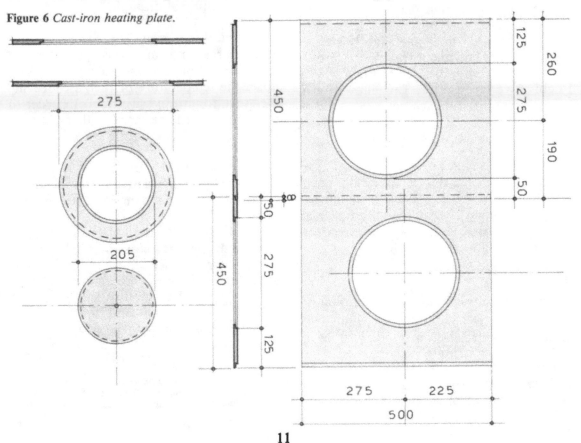

11

Dampers and baffles

Dampers. The input of air and the flow of gases through the stove may be regulated by the use of movable sheet metal plates called 'dampers' situated at the entrances to the stove and chimney. One disadvantage of this system, however, is that it is not conducive to efficient combustion of fuels as it admits ambient air directly into the firebox, which cools the gases. It also takes some time to instruct ladies in developing countries in their correct use.

Baffles. The flow of gases through a stove should be continuous and uninterrupted like a steady stream of water. However, for maximum efficiency it is important to retain the heat generated, for as long as possible, in close proximity to the cooking pots. This may be achieved by means of obstacles called 'baffles'. One particularly efficient method of deriving maximum benefit from the heat in a stove is to provoke a whirl, or vortex, of gases around the cooking pot. This is easier to achieve in stoves with more than one hole for pots. For example, if two pots are to be used it suffices to place one hole slightly to the right of centre and one slightly to the left — see Figure 6 and the description of the Pogbi stove on page 37. This allows for a heat current around each pot.

It is also important to slow down the flow of gases before they leave the stove. One way of achieving this is to direct them downwards before they enter the chimney. This method has the additional advantage of creating a space where chimney deposits may accumulate and be removed.

The chimney

Apart from allowing for the evacuation of gases into the atmosphere, the main function of the chimney is to promote a **draught**, which may be thought of as a 'motor' to facilitate combustion. In technical language a draught may be defined as the **differential between the density of the ambient air and that of the** **hot gases in the chimney.** In an efficient stove this differential will be neither too large nor too small.

Differential too small. The differential will be too small, and the stove will cease to function correctly, **if the temperature of the gases in the chimney is too low.** In this respect stove designers are faced with a frustrating dilemma. On the one hand it is important to retain the maximum amount of heat in the stove in order to warm the cooking pots. Any hot air which escapes to the chimney is obviously wasted for this purpose. On the other hand, however, it is necessary to sacrifice a certain amount of hot gases in order to maintain adequate draught and to avoid the accumulation of tar.[10] In small cooking stoves, the temperature of the gases emitted through the chimney at the normal rate of combustion should not fall below 100°C (measured in mid-chimney). In many developing countries, with particularly hot climates, it is necessary to maintain an even higher temperature in the chimney in order to ensure optimal draught.

Differential too large. The differential will be too large, and cause wastage of heat, if the combustion becomes too intense and raises the temperature of the gases leaving the stove to an excessive level. In order to counter this, it is necessary either:
— to slow down combustion
or
— to regulate the stream of hot gases through properly designed duct sections, or by means of a damper.

If a damper is used, **it must never completely close the stove section** but must always leave space for the continuous evacuation of gases, which may include highly toxic carbon monoxide (CO).

Checking the chimney. A good method is to light a piece of paper and place it inside the cold stove just at the entrance to the

10. Tar condenses in a chimney in the form of creosote, a dark, gluey and highly inflammable substance which, if allowed to accumulate, may cause a chimney fire.

12

chimney. If the burning paper and ashes fly up the chimney, the draught is satisfactory. Several factors — including, for instance, local air turbulence — may give rise to serious difficulties with regard to the proper evacuation of smoke. Solving such problems is a real test of the stove maker's professional capacities (indeed, many failures in this respect may partly explain the pejorative meaning accorded in the French language to the name of the profession). The key to the solution lies in finding the most appropriate means of increasing the draught. This may be achieved, for example, by increasing the height of the chimney or by adding the correct cowl.

Diameter of the chimney. The optimal diameter of any chimney will depend on its height and the heat output in kcal/h of the fire-box. For family-size cooking stoves a fairly small diameter of 10 to 12 cm is generally sufficient and will ensure a steady draught.

Height of the chimney. The most important criterion is that the chimney should be perpendicular to the stove and at least half a metre above the highest point of the roof of the building in which the stove is situated. Thus, under the conditions prevailing in developing countries, a chimney height of approximately 2 m to 3 m should prove adequate. In the case of small stoves, particularly those which are taken in and out of premises, half a metre is sufficient.

Construction of chimneys. Brick or clay chimneys lose less heat, maintain a higher temperature, accumulate less tar and, generally, give better performance than those made out of metal.

A convenient means of constructing chimneys is to use **segments** made out of specially prepared clay (see page 28 "Preparation of clay"). This method uses a mould, 30 × 30 cm at the base and 50 cm high, which can be made with four planks. A metal pipe, of 10 cm diameter, is placed

in the centre of the mould which is then filled with clay. Each lump of clay should be placed around the pipe and well kneaded and pressed to eliminate air pockets. During this process, measurements should be taken at regular intervals to ensure that the pipe is maintained exactly in the middle of the mould. When the clay is hard enough the pipe and planks are removed to leave a hollow chimney segment which has good stability and good heat insulation properties.

The construction of chimney segments.

Cleaning chimneys. It is important to clean chimneys at regular intervals. The frequency will depend upon the rate at which soot and tar accumulate. Chimney cleaning is mandatory in developed countries, due largely to the insistence of fire insurance companies. In the Third World the burning of poor quality wood often causes soot to accumulate very rapidly, and chimneys should be swept more often as a consequence. With fairly small stoves the chimneys may be readily cleaned from above using weighted, coiled

13

wire brushes. This kind of brush can and should be produced locally and made available to stove makers in developing countries. It is also essential to train local people as chimney sweeps in order to ensure that stoves continue to function efficiently at all times.

The cowl

The chimney should be topped with a cowl, of the same diameter and made from metal sheet, which offers protection against rain and improves the draught. This is particularly important for wood-saving stoves.

An efficient chimney cap or cowl, made out of scrap metal, which increases draught regardless of wind direction is shown in Figure 7. In order to ensure correct functioning the first cone should slightly overlap the top of the chimney pipe.

General proportions of stove components

All the components described in this section must together constitute a homogenous entity. For this reason, it is essential that their comparative proportions be respected. **Thus, a change in the dimensions of any element must, in every case, be accompanied by a proportional change in the dimensions of all the other basic components of the stove.** This rule is particularly important when stove designs are being adapted to meet prevailing conditions. For example, in areas where there is good quality firewood, the size of the fire-box may be scaled down. On the other hand the size of the fire-box

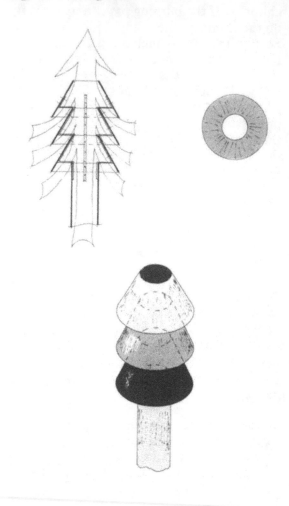

Figure 7 *Chimney cowl.*

may need to be increased in regions where bulky fuel, such as bundles of hay or straw, is commonly used. The above considerations explain why the building of stoves must be considered as a profession, as well as an art, in which proficiency may only be increased through continuous striving to build better and better models.

14

PART TWO

COOKING POTS, ALTERNATIVE FUELS AND COOKING METHODS

J. Cooking pots

If real fuel saving is to be achieved, it is important to pay careful attention to the design of the cooking pots that are to be used on the stove. Ideally, the pot should be lowered into the fire-box in order to present the **largest possible heating surface** and thus derive the maximum benefit from the heat generated. This was the practice in Europe and North America, where cooking pots for wood-burning stoves were usually equipped with rims which supported the pot on the heating plate and prevented air from penetrating the fire-box. Usually they were made of cast-iron which is a strong, durable material with a high thermic inertia.[11]

Cast-iron pots, however, are usually too expensive for poor rural communities and aluminium, which is now increasingly used in developed countries, is the most convenient and suitable substitute. Production presents no problems as standardised pots may be manufactured, at no additional cost, by those local firms which already supply traditional models.

The most common traditional pots in India, Pakistan and East Africa are made from aluminium. Thin sheets, about 1.0 mm or 20 gauge, are spun into the required shape, while thicker sheets are formed with presses. In both cases it is necessary first to manufacture a hard-steel mould. The pots are usually produced in sets of fourteen, starting with 33.5 cm diameter and descending to 19.5 cm. The pots fit into each other and may thus be stacked together.

Attention should also be given to the manufacturing of pot lids. These should be easy to handle and allow vapour to condense, thereby returning water to the pot and preventing leakage, as well as saving energy — see discussion on Community stoves on pages 62 to 70.

The pots described in this section are already being manufactured in Kenya and Pakistan. Wherever possible, quality should be further improved by using thicker aluminium sheets.

Dimensions of cooking pots. The openings of heating plates should be equipped with rings to take different sizes of pot. The pots should be standardised and made rather large. Indeed, the larger the pot the better the heat absorption and the greater the fuel economy of the stove. In view of this, it is suggested that no more than two sizes of pot be used. It is quite acceptable to cook small amounts of food in a large pot as this process gives rise to significant savings in fuel.

The importance of well-designed pots to better cooking and fuel economy often escapes the attention of people who do not themselves cook. It is, indeed, difficult for non-cooks to appreciate the suffering caused to women by badly designed pots which, in addition, do not recuperate the maximum of heat from scarce fuels. It should be stressed, however, that all the stoves presented in this booklet will also function well with most of the aluminium pots available on local markets in developing countries. The principal requirement is that the pots should possess (as most do) a rim.

Figure 8 shows a traditional cast-iron pot together with the aluminium pots designed specifically for the stoves presented in this

11. The flat-bottomed cooking pots which are used in developed countries became fashionable in less energy conscious times and were primarily intended for use on **gas or electric stoves**. It is interesting to note that, with the advent of gas and electric stoves, public utility corporations in industrialised countries popularised the new cooking methods by offering attractive prices for old wood-burning stoves which they replaced with gas or electric models on advantageous terms. The following winter this rapid changeover was deeply regretted by many people who found that, in the absence of their trusty wood-burning stoves, their kitchens had become cold and damp. Encouragingly, wood-burning stoves are coming back into fashion in European regions with a plentiful supply of firewood. In conjunction with this trend, rimmed pots which can be lowered into the fire-box may gain in popularity once more.

booklet. Naturally, the shape of the pot may be modified to suit local conditions — for example, some communities may prefer to use pots with rounded rather than square bottoms.

Figure 8 *Traditional European cast-iron pot and a newly-designed aluminium pot.*

The author displaying a cast-iron heating plate equipped with an efficient, properly designed cooking pot.

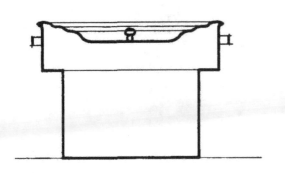

Heat absorption. That part of the pot which is in direct contact with the fire soon becomes black. This surface absorbs heat well and **does not need to be cleaned** unless, due to faulty combustion, it becomes covered with a layer of tar which will insulate the pot and reduce efficiency. This will rarely be the case if the pots are correctly used on the stove models presented in this booklet. For easy cleaning, some women smear the cold pots with a liquid mixture of clay and ashes.

K. Alternative fuels

Unfortunately, many fuels such as electricity or bottled gas, which could eventually be used as alternatives to firewood in areas where wood shortage is most acute, are at present beyond the means of poor rural communities — especially when distribution expenses and cost and maintenance of equipment are taken into account. Other energy sources — such as biogas and solar energy — are only in the early stages of development, and more patient effort will be required before they may be used on a massive scale.

In the meantime, however, considerable savings in the use of firewood may be achieved by encouraging techniques which make greater use of abundant materials such as shrubs, twigs, bark, straw, hay, weeds, dry leaves, rural waste and combustible municipal garbage.

Bundles and faggots

The major drawback with the above-mentioned materials is that they all burn too quickly to be used for cooking purposes. This difficulty can, however, be overcome if they are made into bundles, or small faggots. This process diminishes the access of air and thereby slows combustion. Efficiency can be further enhanced if each

Figure 9 *Simple devices for pressing bundles and faggots.*

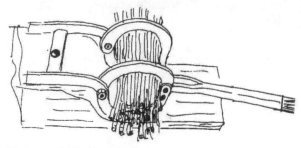

b) A metal 'fork' press

a) Pressing bundles with a rope and stick

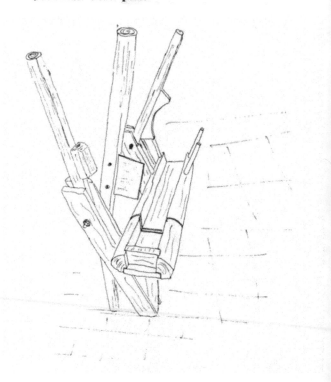

c) A 'baker' press for larger bundles

d) A wood press with guillotine for cutting bundles

bundle or faggot contains a piece of wood at its centre. During combustion these pieces of wood will change into glowing embers on the grate, pre-heating the primary air and generally maintaining a high temperature in the fire-box.

Bundles may be fashioned very simply by hand, but their heat value increases if they are pressed using simple devices, such as those illustrated — which were among those demonstrated in 1980 at the "Wood for Survival" exhibition organised by the author, under the auspices of the Bellerive Foundation, in the grounds of the United Nations office at Geneva.

Bundles and faggots should not be looked upon merely as a poor wood substitute. Indeed, for many uses they are even **more suitable** than larger pieces of firewood. For example, bakers traditionally use faggots composed of branches of between 3 and 5 cm in diameter to heat bread ovens.

18

Briquettes

In towns and villages alike there is a vast quantity of waste material — including dry weeds, husks, cotton waste, coconut fibre, olive residue, fish waste, wood shavings, sawdust and municipal garbage — that may be converted into excellent fuel if shredded into small particles and pressed into briquettes with the aid of special machines capable of exerting a pressure of about 1,000 kg per cm^2. Rural and urban populations can, however, compress all available waste quite adequately with the aid of simple hand-operated presses.

Paper ball briquettes. Useful briquettes may be made by hand by pressing well soaked newspapers into the shape of tennis balls. The resulting briquette will be even harder if the newspapers are sprinkled with wood ash before being compressed. In Switzerland during the Second World War paper ball briquettes were made with the aid of a simple two-handled press similar to that shown in Figure 10.[12] As can be seen from the illustration, the lower arm of the press was fixed to a wooden board. The pressure exerted varied from 50 to 100 kg (or 5 to 10 kg/cm²) depending on the size of the ball (the paper balls become increasingly difficult to compress as their size is increased).

Binders. A binder is a sort of glue (preferably combustible) which is compressed with the briquettes in order to prevent it from falling apart. With industrial presses exerting high pressure, binders are not necessary and may even

hinder the proper functioning of the machine. This is not the case, however, with simple hand presses. Resin, tar, fish waste, certain plants,[13] sewage mud and, if necessary, cow dung[14] are all suitable binding materials.

When dealing with highly calorific waste, such as charcoal dust which needs a particularly strong binder, the use of **non-combustible** binders such as clay, mud or slime may be justified as a **last resort**.[15] However, it is more advisable to mix the charcoal dust with organic waste which gives a higher heat value.

Preparing the materials. The first operation is the **chopping of the chosen material** for which the most suitable tool is a machete or broad axe. For production on a somewhat larger scale, a hand-operated straw chopper (still widely used in some parts of Europe) may be employed. Materials such as charcoal may be **crushed** into small pieces or a coarse powder in a wooden mortar. Once chopped, the material may be soaked in water for about 24 hours to render it more elastic and amenable to the manufacture of briquettes.

The next step is to press water out of the mass and to blend in suitable binding materials. Adding used motor oil to the mixture increases heat value, but tends to make the briquettes crumble. It thus acts as an **anti-binder** and should be used sparingly, if at all.

12. Paper rollers, producing hard newspaper rolls suitable for burning in household hearths, are still found in many European countries, such as the 'Rol-Buche' produced by Godin S.A. in France.
13. Algae were successfully used as binding material in Swiss towns during the First World War.
14. The use of animal manure is **not** to be encouraged **and must be avoided whenever possible**, as this precious material forms part of a natural cycle which should not be disturbed. Quite apart from the ecological consequences, the burning of dung is also a major cause of eye and lung disease in developing countries.
15. Briquettes made in this way are available in certain African towns, including Nairobi. Their heat value is relatively small (around 1,000 kcal/kg) and the ash content high. However, they do have the merit of usefully employing waste substances that would normally be discarded.

Figure 10 *Simple paper ball press.*

Transparent plastic bags, which burn well and give off no noxious gases, may prove a welcome addition. **However, great care should be taken not to burn plastics containing chlorine or any other substances which could be harmful to health.**

Next it is necessary to **compress** the materials from which the briquettes are to be made. Few waste materials can be moulded into satisfactory briquettes merely with the hands, and it is usually necessary to have recourse to some form of press.

Hand press. The manual press illustrated in Figures 11 and 12 is just one example of the variety of manual presses that have recently been designed and built in Switzerland. Certain of the presses have already been field-tested in developing countries.

Figure 11 *Hand press.*

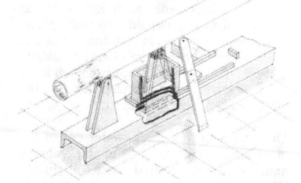

Figure 12b *Front section.*

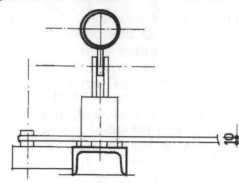

Figure 12c *Top section.*

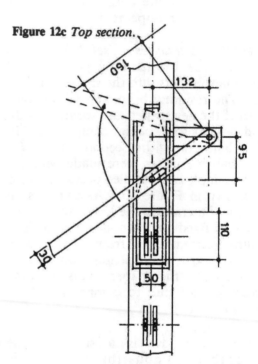

Figure 12a *Design of the hand press — side section.*

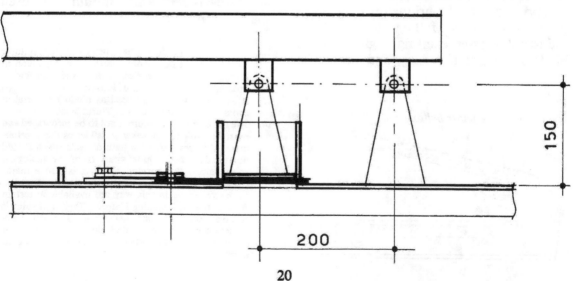

20

As can be seen from the illustrations, the press is made of a salvaged "u"-shaped steel bar in which there is a square **opening** covered by a **movable plate**. Built over the opening is a **square box** (11 cm long, 5.5 cm broad and 7 cm high) into which the materials to be compressed are placed. A **lever** is attached to two supports which are welded to the base bar. This lever works a **pressure plate** which enters the square box and compresses the briquette. The lever is then raised and the movable plate at the bottom of the square box is pushed aside, allowing the briquettes to be forced out of the box.

The press exerts a pressure of over 500 kg or about 10 kg/cm^2. The lever is made out of 2 inch steel pipe and can be **extended** by means of a wooden pole to further increase the pressure. Satisfactory briquettes were made with this press by the author in Nairobi in February 1981. The heat values recorded by these sample briquettes are given in Table 1.

The higher the pressure that can be exerted by the press, the higher the density and heat value of the resulting briquettes. Thus, wherever possible, it is desirable to use equipment capable of producing high pressure. It is possible, for example, considerably to increase pressure, and reduce physical effort, by resort to simple hydraulic presses. Obviously this would involve more cost, but the quality of the briquettes would be significantly improved.

Earth block press. Such a machine is a manually operated piston press which was initially developed[16] for making earth

16. By the Inter-American Housing and Planning Centre (CINVA) in Colombia.

Table 1. Technical characteristics of briquettes

Type	Composition	Humidity	Ash %	Net heat value in kcal/kg	Remarks
Waste paper balls pressed by hand	Paper soaked in water and powdered with wood ash	6.9	2.9	3,825	—
Straw and cow dung pressed by hand	50% manure 50% straw	5.4	9.5	3,599	—
Charcoal dust and clay pressed by hand	—	—	73	975	Briquette found in Nairobi market
Rural waste pressed by hand	Hay, dry leaves, wood shavings, charcoal dust, 10% cow manure	8.0	19.0	3,502	Briquette made in Nairobi
Rural waste pressed on Terstaram press	40% straw 40% sawdust 20% manure	9.2	14.0	3,266	—
Rural waste pressed on Terstaram press	30-45% chopped twigs, 30-45% charcoal dust & 15-20% cow manure	2.4	32.2	4,408	High content of ash is probably due to sand present in charcoal

Source: Laboratory tests carried out by the Research and Development Centre for Energy Economy in Warsaw.

building blocks out of a mixture of soil and cement. This press, which is known as the Cinva Ram, can be readily converted to produce excellent briquettes from agricultural waste simply by **reducing the dimensions of the compression box** with the aid of wooden boards. The press is then capable of producing briquettes of about 5 cm in height. The length and width of the briquettes will remain the same as for building blocks but, once thoroughly dry,[17] they can easily be broken into smaller pieces as required.

The author and Mr Haas demonstrating the use of a hand press for making briquettes.

Industrial presses. The industrial presses currently available are capable of exerting a pressure of about 1,000 kg/cm². The combination of high pressure and the heat generated during the compression process breaks down the elasticity of the materials used and enables hard, solid briquettes to be produced **without the need for a binder** which would only hinder the functioning of the machine.

The capacity of industrial presses ranges from about 100 to 3,000 kg/h. The press itself is only one element in a complete **production chain** which will usually include a grinder, a drier and a packing machine.

L. Other fuels

Kerosene

There are regions in the world where firewood shortage is so pronounced that consumption must be stopped altogether, pending the successful completion of programmes to replenish fuel stocks with new trees and fast-growing shrubs.

For such regions one must consider fuels other than wood, or even wood waste, to cook and to heat premises. One such fuel is kerosene, known in some countries as paraffin.

Research on the optimal use of kerosene was commenced during the last century by the Polish engineer, Ignacy Lukasiewicz, who in 1853 introduced the distillation of crude oil and invented the first kerosene lamp. The lamp worked with a wick which was partly immersed in kerosene. The fuel gradually soaked through to the top of the wick where the flame could be applied and receive the requisite input of oxygen.

This principle was also applied to cooking stoves and heating appliances. Kerosene lamps are still used today and render appreciable service in many parts of the world. Also, kerosene appliances working on the basis of wicks immersed in kerosene are still in use both in developing and developed countries. However, wick-type cooking stoves are now rare, as fuel efficiency is not very good and the stoves tend to give off smoke and unpleasant smelling fumes.

The best means of cooking on kerosene is to introduce air into the fuel and vaporise it before combustion. The first stove using this principle was designed by F.W. Lindquist in Sweden in 1880. The manufacture of his stoves was commenced

17. Drying increases the heat value of the briquettes and thus economises fuel. Ideally, briquettes should be produced well in advance of use so as to allow for thorough drying.

on an industrial scale in Stockholm in 1892 under the brand name "Primus". Ever since these stoves have given good service all over the world, and there are no reasons why they should not continue to give the same good service in regions deprived of wood or other fuels.

Basically, the stove consists of a pressure-proofed tank equipped with a hand-driven pump which serves to introduce air. Kerosene mixed with air enters a pre-heated pipe, attains its boiling point (150 to 230°C, depending on the quality) and changes into vapour. The vapour leaves the pipe via a calibrated jet and, when lit, produces a strong flame which receives additional oxygen from the ambient air.

Primus-type stoves (as is the case with all implements operating with a flame) are not devoid of danger. This, however, arises principally out of faulty operation rather than inherent design faults (which can easily be remedied). In particular, the primus-type stove will only function correctly with **clean** kerosene, a commodity which is often rare in poor households. If the kerosene contains impurities the jet will become blocked. Indeed, even when pure kerosene is being used it is necessary to clean the jet daily with the special needles supplied with each stove. In addition it is essential to pre-heat the burners properly before lighting the stove. If this is not done the primus may become flooded with kerosene — thereby augmenting the risk of fire.

Such problems are not, however, insuperable and should not preclude increased resort to primus-type stoves in regions where there is no wood. However, there is one serious obstacle to the promotion of primus-type stoves, namely their price. Pressure-proved tanks must be properly manufactured, the hand-driven pump calls for precision working, and the burner must be produced in a well-equipped workshop. All this is reflected in the price which is normally too high for the poor people who are the first victims of

firewood shortage. Also, the price of kerosene may constitute an obstacle.

In co-operation with the author, Mr Emil Haas, a retired Swiss stove expert, carried out research to reduce the price of kerosene burners. This resulted in a new model, presented in Figure 13, which represents a departure from the "wick" and "primus" principles. The new equipment consists of a container (which could, for example, be an old food can) filled with clean kerosene and placed about 70 to 100 cm above the burner. The kerosene flows from the container through a copper pipe with an inner diameter of 4 mm. The flow is regulated by a valve situated just below the container. At its lower end the pipe is twisted into a coil shape and welded to a second copper pipe, with an inner diameter of 8 mm. This pipe is twisted through one and one half turns and closed at the other end. Three holes for jets are then pierced in the lower pipe. The upper coiled pipe, or 'basket', is supported on a tripod over a circular metal plate in which alcohol or kerosene may be lit to pre-heat the basket.

As soon as the basket has been pre-heated to the boiling point of kerosene, the valve may be opened to allow the kerosene to descend from the container by gravity. It flows round the coils of the basket where it is transformed into vapour under pressure. This vapour then enters the thicker pipe, where the pressure is somewhat diminished, and is forced out through the jets. When lit the vapour produces flames which attain 700 to 800°C. Combustion of the kerosene is better than on the wick stoves but less satisfactory than on a primus-type. When the burner is hot, no noticeable amount of smoke escapes from the chimney of the stove in which it is being used. This indicates that most of the combustible volatiles have been properly burned.

The principal merits of the new burner are its simplicity for production purposes and its relatively low price. An additional advantage is that, in one simple movement, the burner may be placed in any of the

Figure 13 *Kerosene burner*

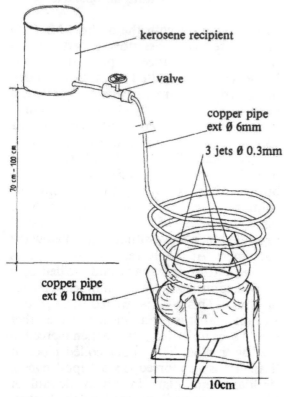

kerosene recipient

valve

copper pipe
ext Ø 6mm

3 jets Ø 0.3mm

70 cm – 100 cm

copper pipe
ext Ø 10mm

10cm

stoves presented in this publication, thus substituting kerosene for firewood. The burner may also be used to fire the hot air generator described below.

However, while the burner functions well in experienced hands it is subject, at its present stage of development, to many of the reservations that apply to primus-type stoves. In particular, the kerosene must be clean and the container free from dust and dirt. Users must also be thoroughly trained in the correct use of the system. This will involve instruction in the pre-heating of the burners, the daily cleaning of the jets and the proper use of the valve which regulates the flow of kerosene into the burner. All these drawbacks may be overcome with time, but they require further efforts and investigations which are currently being undertaken by Mr Haas and the author.*

*At the time of printing, new models have been developed and tested with good results. They will be presented in the specialized press and in future editions of this book.

Diesel oil

The technology needed for the efficient use of this fuel is well established and in daily use in all developed as well as in many developing countries. The fuel itself is, of course, available wherever there are routes used by trucks. A source of electric power is needed to ensure the proper combustion of diesel oil. This may be obtained either from the mains grid or from a generator. Electric power is needed to mix the oil with air and eject it under the required pressure. When lit, the oil/air mixture gives a good flame which may be used for baking as well as for community cooking.

Bottled gas

Some developing countries suffering from a pronounced shortage of firewood do possess deposits of natural gas. Others hope to discover such deposits. Natural gas is an excellent fuel both for cooking and baking. Larger towns may be supplied through municipal mains. Natural gas can also be liquefied and sold in bottles. The exploitation of natural gas and its distribution calls for considerable funds and organisational effort. However, the price of gas, in terms of calorific value, is already lower than the price of firewood in some developing countries. Elsewhere it may be a sound policy to supply bottled gas on a large scale and to plant forests intensively in order eventually to achieve a better ecological equilibrium.

Biogas

The large-scale distribution of bottled gas among poor communities may still be a remote and somewhat ambitious proposal. The local production of biogas from available organic waste, however, is of much more immediate relevance. Production of biogas in warm climates calls for a relatively small investment as the temperature of the fermenting mass can be maintained at about 30°C without insulation and without the use of external energy sources.

There is no shortage of biogas installations

which have been thoroughly tested and which give satisfactory performance. The problem is that they cost more than poor communities can afford, and that they are usually difficult to operate and maintain. The best known models work on manure diluted in water, and are common in China and India. This calls for a supply of water and some hydraulic arrangements, which increase the cost of the units. Storage of the digested liquid presents additional problems. Nevertheless such installations have a proven track record and should be installed wherever the necessary conditions are found.

However, countries where the shortage of firewood is particularly acute are often located in dry regions where there is little water and rarely enough cattle manure. Often the only organic material available in sufficient quantities is dry cellulose in the form of hay, straw or dry leaves.

Thus, the author has developed a biogas installation which is particularly suited to warm, dry countries. Basically it consists of two plastic sheets. The first sheet is spread on the ground and kept within a square frame about 30 cm high. A heap of manure is built up on the sheet in the middle of the frame. The heap is moistened with several buckets of water so that the base stays in the slurry. The sheet-lined frame serves as a basin. Another sheet covers the heap of manure and is fixed to the bottom of the frame. The slurry forms a hydraulic seal and the gas is collected by a pipe fixed in the middle of the upper sheet.

A detailed description of this installation is to be published shortly in a separate booklet.

If the necessary materials are prepared in advance the installation may be erected within a day. The first family-size model was erected in Kenya in August 1981. Another larger model was built in January 1983, also in Kenya. Both models have withstood the climatic conditions quite

well. The heap of manure gives methane gas for over a year.

The model described above, together with many others, enables biogas to be one of the important alternatives to firewood in many developing countries.

M. Hay boxes

Hay boxes are useful fuel saving devices which are an important part of an efficient cooking system. They are very simple to arrange and can be made in no time out of, for example, an old box (see Figure 14).

Figure 14 *Hay box.*

A good idea is to use a straw basket equipped with a lid and filled with insulating material such as dry hay, straw, dry leaves, wood shavings or crumpled newspaper. A nest is formed in this material to accommodate the pot. To avoid pieces of insulating material falling into the food, the nest may be lined with a piece of rag or cloth tucked in at the sides of the box.

For cooking it is not necessary to heat many foods to boiling point. A temperature of 85°C is usually quite sufficient. Thus, as soon as the food **starts** to boil the cooking pot should be transferred, in one quick movement, to the hay box nest and covered with an old pillow filled with insulating material.

Once inside the hay box, food will cook thoroughly and remain hot for several hours. Certainly, there will be no need to re-heat the evening meal for the benefit of those returning home late.

Figure 15 *Cross-section of hay box.*

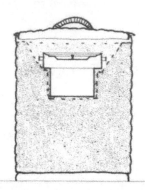

Testing efficiency. The simplest means of testing the efficiency, and proper functioning, of a hay box is to touch the outside walls about half an hour after a hot cooking pot has been placed in the nest. If the box is warm, it means that the insulating material is inadequate and should be increased or replaced.

Improving efficiency. To further improve the efficiency of the hay box, a hot, flat stone or brick may be placed at the bottom of the nest. This will serve as an improvised hotplate and will keep the food warm within the hay box for an even longer period.

Care must be taken not to spill food when the pot is placed in the box as hay and straw cease to be good insulating materials when wet.

Some experimentation is advisable in order to obtain the best results from hay boxes. For instance, at higher altitudes, where water boils at temperatures lower than 100°C, it will be more difficult to maintain the temperature in the box above 85°C.

N. Cooking methods

Short-term versus long-term cooking

The theory has been advanced that even if some stoves are less efficient than a well-managed open fire for the purposes of **short-term** cooking, they present advantages in **long-term** cooking. This is not, however, a valid argument. In countries and regions where there is a shortage of firewood there can be no justification for long-term cooking. With improved cooking methods, such as the pre-soaking of dry foodstuffs (e.g. peas, beans, or cereals), cutting food into small pieces and the correct use of hay boxes, all meals may be prepared in a relatively short time. Certainly, for most foods there is no need for cooking periods which exceed one hour.

This reasoning aside, there is no logical reason to suppose that stoves that are efficient for short-term cooking should be any less so for long-term cooking. If such should prove to be the case, the stove in question should be redesigned or discarded.

The cooking system

The above remarks illustrate the importance of promoting a **complete cooking system** to complement the deployment of fuel-efficient stoves. Equal attention must be given to all the component parts of the system which include the promotion of alternative fuels, well designed cooking pots, more rational cooking methods, simple fuel saving devices such as hay boxes, the use of dry wood cut into small pieces and the proper management of the fire. If introduced simultaneously and used in conjunction with modern stoves, the above measures form a **comprehensive package deal**. Through this it is possible to achieve truly spectacular economies in fuel wood, reducing consumption to as little as one tenth of existing levels. Another integral part of the package deal must be the planting of fast-growing trees and shrubs to replenish forest reserves, thereby reversing the ecological catastrophe that threatens many regions of the world which depend upon wood for survival. We have the means; what is needed now is the will.

PART THREE

DESCRIPTION, CONSTRUCTION AND TESTING OF STOVE AND OVEN MODELS

O. Preparation of clay

The suitability of clay for stove building has been acknowledged for centuries all over the world. It is difficult to give advice on the preparation of clay that will be accurate in all cases, however. This is because there are many different types of clay, and their individual properties vary considerably according to factors such as geographical location and geological formation.

An empirical approach is thus called for, and the best advice is to discuss the problem with local potters and brick-makers who are usually thoroughly acquainted with the particular characteristics of the local clay. The clay used in brick manufacture is usually fairly light — what the French call 'l'argile maigre' — and is, therefore, in the majority of cases suitable for stove manufacture. If, however, it is slightly on the heavy side ('trop grasse'), it should first be mixed with sand.

One test is of particular relevance when examining the respective qualities of different types of clay: small balls of each type should be made and heated to a high temperature in a fire-box or forge. If the ball becomes hard, the clay is suitable for stove making. If it crumbles it should be rejected, and the search for better varieties of clay continued.

Deposits of good clay are valuable natural resources. Their exploitation should, therefore, be properly managed and conducted in consultation with the local authorities. In particular, the clay should only be dug from layers where there are no plant roots or other vegetable residues. Access roads should be provided to link the deposits to the various work sites, and freshly dug clay should be left for some time in the open air, exposed to the elements, until it becomes more malleable and easier to work. If large quantities are required it is advisable to first dry the clay, crush it into powder and then soak it for a few days before use. If only small quantities are needed it is usually possible to obtain, from a brick factory, clay that has already been well prepared and kneaded, ready for the production of raw bricks.

Resistance to thermic shocks

During the cooking process clay undergoes considerable thermic shocks and, unless specially treated to render it more fire resistant, may well crack and crumble. To avoid this a common procedure is to mix chopped straw, cow dung, wood ashes, grain husks, charcoal dust or other

The author shows how difficult it is to tear apart a bundle of hay.

28

ingredients into the clay at the preparation stage. Every potter develops his own mixture, using readily available materials plus water. Once mixed and kneaded the clay is left in a container for between one and seven days until it matures and assumes the consistency of bread dough.

'Grogging'

To render the clay even more suitable for the construction of stoves and braziers it should be 'grogged', which is the term used to describe the addition of crushed, baked bricks, crushed tiles or ceramic waste which is first sieved into particles the size of medium semolina. The result is a fire-resistant clay known in French as 'chamotte'. Usually a mixture containing 10 to 30% grog is sufficient but, again depending on the quality of the local clay, there may be cases where smaller or larger proportions could be envisaged.

The hay method

Once again a study of the methods used in the past in Europe brings to light another excellent process which uses hay to make the body of a stove solid and resistant to thermic shocks. The method is mentioned in the section dealing with bread ovens in the first French encyclopaedia, which was published under the direction of Denis Diderot during the 18th century.[18] The technique was revived and tested, with excellent results, by Pierre Delacrétaz of Lausanne — a distinguished specialist in the construction of bread ovens.[19] Each stem of hay used should be about 1.0 mm in diameter and at least 30 cm long (i.e. about the length of the forearm from fist to elbow). The stems, which should be straight and strong, are formed into bundles 3 to 5 cm in diameter and carefully kneaded and pounded into the grogged clay — in a proportion of 1:1 — until a homogeneous, 'plastic' mass is formed, similar to that used for pottery. If the mass is too humid or plastic it is easier to work, but shrinks rapidly during the drying stage, leaving cracks and, in many cases, altering the basic dimensions of the stove.

The above process requires some effort, but, once dry, the resulting material withstands heat extremely well. As the author demonstrates in the photograph, it is not humanly possible to tear apart a bundle of hay of the dimensions used in this process. When incorporated into clay the hay acts like the iron rods in reinforced concrete, strengthening the structure and preventing it from crumbling. Indeed, bread ovens manufactured with this material in France were noted for their durability.

Should any cracks appear, however, they should be moistened with water and then filled with the same clay as used for construction. The finished stove body should never be smeared with clay for aesthetic effect as the clay will not adhere to the surface. A more satisfactory, and equally pleasing, solution is to coat the stove with reddish, sandy soil that has been well diluted with water.

Circular shapes. When the mixture is to be used for constructing flat forms the hay may be mashed into the clay at will. However, for circular shapes — such as fire-box walls, chimneys and the like — the stems should remain unbroken so as to make long coils of reinforced clay, curved at the ends, which make the structure even stronger. Once again, the consistency of the coils should be plastic and fairly dense. When used for constructing stoves they should, whenever possible, be literally **thrown** into place (some splashing of clay is inevitable) and thoroughly kneaded with the hands and fingers to eliminate air pockets in the mass.

P. Stove models

The well-managed open fire (WMOF)

There is a popular and widespread belief that, when cooking by open fire, it is only possible to recover about 3 to 10% of the

18. See — *Encyclopédie, ou Dictionnaire Raisonné des Sciences, des Arts et des Métiers.*
19. See — *Les Vieux Fours à Pain*, P. Delacrétaz, Editions de la Thièle, Yverdon, Switzerland.

heat value of the firewood used. This estimate is perhaps well founded when cooking is conducted in the open air, unprotected from the wind, and using large pieces of, often damp, wood. However, if the fire is well shielded from the elements and fed with small pieces of dry wood, and if the pot is positioned in the midst of the flames, there is no reason why a fuel-efficiency rate of between 15 to 20% should not be attained. This rate, incidentally, is higher than that obtained on a great number of stoves currently being promoted in developing countries. It may, thus, be more logical to re-appraise open-fire cooking, with a view to improving its efficiency, before attempting to design new stoves.

It is suggested that the 18 to 20% fuel-efficiency rate that it is possible to achieve under field conditions with a well-managed open fire should be considered as the minimum requirement for wood-burning

stoves. Models recording lower rates should not be retained for wide-scale promotion as they do not contribute to the conservation of firewood.

Description and construction. The first step is to set a flat stone into the ground. This serves as a base for the fire and as a means to increase the combustion temperature (see Figure 16).

The three stones used in traditional open fire cooking are replaced by three solid conical clay blocks from which ledges are cut so that the pots may sit securely over the fire. The ledges are cut, 3 cm deep and 3 cm high, approximately 14 to 16 cm above ground level. This allows for good stability as well as the minimum of contact between the pot and the clay — thus ensuring optimal heat recuperation. The tops of the clay blocks are slightly higher than the pot placed on the ledges. A stone is placed in each of the gaps between the clay blocks and, once the fire is burning well, these may be pushed closer to the fire in order to reduce heat loss and slightly regulate the inflow of air. The fire should be protected from the wind. As the pots are firmly supported, the housewife is able to turn her face away from the heat and smoke when stirring food. Her comfort may be further increased if the WMOF is built on a stand above ground level.

Figure 16 *Well-managed open fire.*

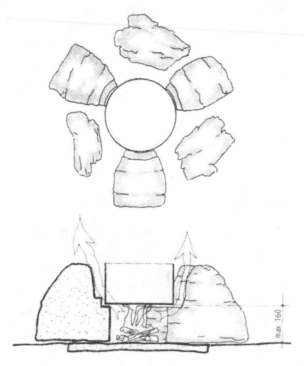

Cooking on a well-managed open fire in Kenya.

30

The blocks of clay should be prepared according to the method already described in section O.

Evaluation and testing. The fuel-efficiency rate of the WMOF (calculated according to the Eindhoven formula — see Section V) varies around 20%. It should be noted that these readings, recorded during field work while using poor quality firewood are significantly lower that those achieved at the University of Eindhoven under laboratory conditions.[20] In conclusion, the fuel-efficiency of open fires varies enormously in the range of, say, 3 to 20%. Thus, frequently heard claims such as "cookstove X consumes Y% less wood than an open fire" are highly misleading and virtually meaningless.

Before contemplating the introduction of new stoves into developing countries, the fuel efficiency rate of each model should be firmly established and compared to that of a WMOF. This should be the main criterion for assessing the value of stoves for wide-scale promotion. The opinion of users with regard to fuel saving should be treated with great caution as women in developing countries are usually prepared to accept any new stove, however inefficient, that removes the need to endure heat and smoke in their faces. Because of this, they are often prepared to defend them by stating that they economise on fuel in relation to an open fire. It should also be remembered that chimney stoves are considered a status symbol and are, consequently, preferred to open fires.

Protected open fire

History. This model was developed as a direct consequence of investigations into open-fire cooking. It is the result of efforts to improve efficiency in the simplest, most inexpensive manner, **through diminishing loss of energy due to radiation and convection.**

Description. The stove consists of an open cylinder made of clay, with a door, ash chamber, grate and fire-box.

Figure 17 *Protected open fire — general view.*

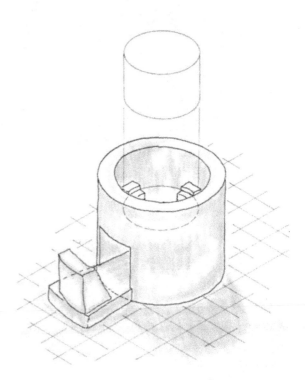

Pots are supported in the stove on three ledges formed on the inner walls of the stove (see Figures 17 and 18). The ledges may be arranged so as to accommodate two different sizes of pot, selected from among those already being used in the particular household.

The ledges are the only parts of the structure which, due to their relative fragility, call for periodic repairs. They may be considerably reinforced, however, if they are constructed from stones or refractory bricks which are well set into the stove walls. An alternative solution is to suspend the pots from metal rings placed on top of the stove.

Construction. The stove is made from clay, prepared as described in Section O. The

20. See: *Some Performance Tests on Open Fires and the Family Cooker*, Technical University of Eindhoven, June 1980; *Some studies on open fires, shielded fires and heavy stoves*, Eindhoven, October 1981. These documents are of considerable relevance to the promotion of fuel-efficient wood stoves.

Moulds for making stove.

Set of moulds ready to be filled with clay.

chamber are then positioned and the cylinder is filled with clay up to the level of the ash chamber. Next the mould for the grate sitting is added, and the fire-box is fashioned by hand in the shape of an inverted cone with three buttresses. 14 cm above grate level, ledges are formed on the buttresses in order to provide a firm emplacement for the cooking pots. Additional ledges are made slightly above in order to permit the use of a larger cooking pot. Cooking pots supported on the lower ledges will be entirely in the stove, and recuperate the maximum of heat. Pots positioned on the upper ledges may be slightly higher than the stove. Between the buttresses, the gap separating the cooking pot and the stove walls should be in the region of 2 cm, so as to allow for the easy exit of gases and optimal heat recovery.

The grate may be conveniently fashioned from iron wire (6 to 8 mm grade) cold

moulds (see photographs) are three pieces of wood, cut respectively in the shape of a door, ash chamber and a sitting for the grate, and a metal cylinder.

The first step is to place the sheet metal cylinder on the stove stand, or on a board, and then fill it with lumps of clay and hay mixture until a layer about 5 cm deep is formed. This constitutes the base of the stove. The moulds for the door and ash

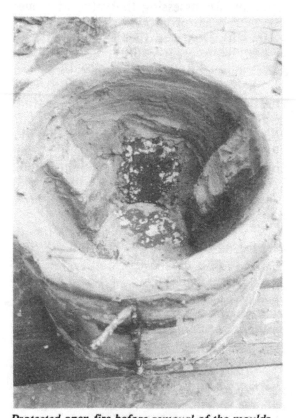

Protected open fire before removal of the moulds.

32

Protected open fire ready for use.

The grate.

hammered into a coil as shown below.

To increase user comfort the stove may be installed on a stand made from stones strengthened with lumps of clay prepared according to the hay method. The stand should be made slightly larger than the base of the stove, so as to form a work top on which pots and cooking utensils may be kept. Sufficient space should also be reserved on the platform, in front of the stove, for a lump of clay. When pushed in or out of the stove opening this regulates the inflow of air.

If it is desired to transport the stove in and out of the household, it should be equipped with sheet metal bands to which handles may be conveniently attached. Alternatively, before the clay dries indentations may be made in the outer walls of the stove, in order to provide hand holds for transportation.

Evaluation. The protected open fire may be used with any cooking pots and the only costs involved are those of local labour and clay, as well as the modest price of a metal grate, which may also be manufactured in the village by local tinsmiths.

The principal advantages of the stove are its low price and the fact that it may replace the traditional open fire without losing thermal efficiency — even in windy conditions.

In addition, its fuel efficiency rate is higher than that of a well-managed open fire. A test conducted under field conditions in Pakistan during October 1983 revealed that it was possible to boil 4.0 litres of water in 17 minutes on 365 gm of wood, i.e. on 91 gm per litre of water boiled. 4.0 litres of water were brought to the boil and kept simmering for 75 minutes on 670 gm of wood. The fuel efficiency rate recorded was 29.5%.[21]

21. The tests were carried out by Mr Muqarrab Khan of the University of Engineering and Technology in Peshawar at noon on 18th October 1983, on a sunny, windless day. The air temperature was 22°C; initial water temperature 24°C. The water boiled at 96°C.

Figure 18 *Top view and cross-section of protected open fire.*

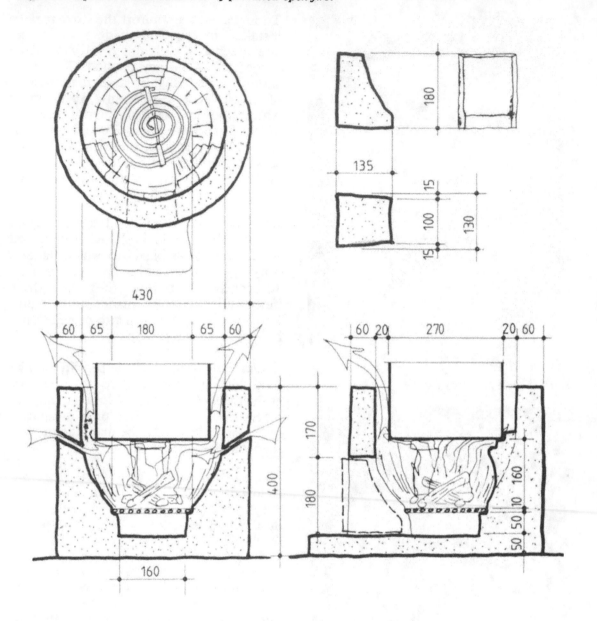

Crescent stove

History. This stove was inspired by research on the Polish brazier. The basic design of both models is similar, but the Crescent stove is constructed from clay rather than metal sheets. It represents the next logical stage, after the well-managed open fire and protected open fire, on the road towards the development of stoves that are both fuel efficient and comfortable to use. In all major respects the stove remains as first described in the first edition of this book. However, new dimensions have been introduced on the basis of experience gained during the past years. The new version uses pots with a capacity of 8 to 9 litres.

Description. In the first English edition it was suggested that the main mould should be a plastic bucket with the bottom cut away. We now feel that it is preferable to use a purpose-designed metal sheet mould, which should be cylindrical rather than

34

conical in form. An added advantage is that the same mould may be employed to construct other stove models as well as the Crescent type.

The dimensions of the stove may, of course, be modified to suit particular local conditions. It is essential, however, to preserve the basic proportions if optimal fuel efficiency is to be maintained.

After a first layer of clay, 5 cm deep, has been placed in the bottom of the cylinder, moulds are inserted for the ash chamber, the door and the grate (see photograph).

The cylinder is then filled to grate height and the fire-box is shaped with the hands in the form of an open cone, according to the designs supplied herein.

A platform, on which the cooking pot will stand, is constructed at the top of the fire-box. It is made in the form of a half-moon, or **crescent** — from which the stove derives its name.

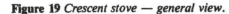
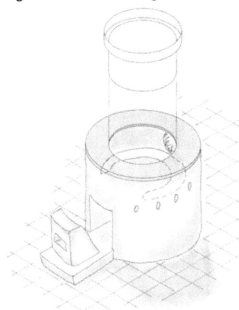

Figure 19 *Crescent stove — general view.*

The walls of the stove are then built up to the top of the cylinder. A mould for a chimney opening is placed in the wall just above the middle section of the crescent-shaped platform.

Crescent stove before removal of the moulds.

Crescent stove at work in a Kenyan village.

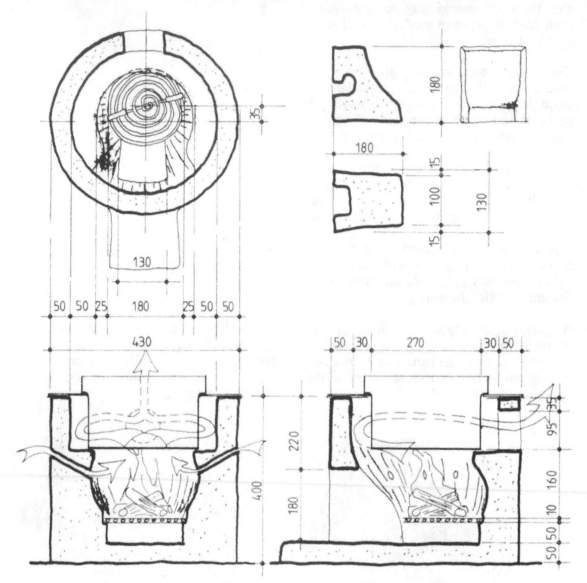

Figure 20 *Top view and cross-section of Crescent stove.*

The stove is covered with a metal sheet ring to protect it from damage when heavy pots are taken in and out (see Figures 19 and 20).

The pots stand on the crescent platform and are supported by their rims on the metal ring. The rims of the pot seal the opening and prevent air from penetrating into the stove.

As can be seen from Figure 20, the flames and hot gases heat the base of the pot and are then forced to flow around the sides

before leaving by the only available exit — the chimney.

Materials. The main material is clay prepared according to the method described above. It is suggested that the grate be made from iron rods as shown in the section dealing with the Protected Open Fire.

The ring could be manufactured from recycled sheet metal.

In order to ensure proper functioning, it is

36

essential that rimmed pots of the correct diameter be used with this stove.

Construction. As indicated above, the stove is formed in a metal sheet cylindrical mould. As soon as the clay is sufficiently firm, the cylinder is opened and the interior moulds removed. In case of difficulty the wooden moulds may be separated from the clay with the aid of a wire or metal blade. Once the moulds have been removed, iron rods or sticks (8 to 10 mm in diameter) are used to make six ducts through the walls of the stove. These will ensure the secondary air supply. The ducts should be started high on the outer walls of the stove and pierced obliquely downwards to penetrate the fire-box just below the crescent platform. With this arrangement, the downward flow of ambient air is increased automatically by a strong fire and diminishes, or ceases altogether, as the fire settles down.

Once built, the stove should be placed in the shade to dry. In very hot, dry climates it is often advisable to cover the stove with wet rugs to prevent the surface from drying too quickly.

The moulds should be removed when the clay is half dry and then thoroughly washed, dried and smeared with oil or fat in readiness for the next stove.

If all the moulds and the clay are carefully prepared in advance, construction of the stove should take no longer than one hour. It will be ready for use three or four days later and the clay will be baked during the cooking process.

The chimney may either be constructed using segments placed next to the stove — manufactured according to the method described on page 13 — or from metal pipe.

If the stove is to be used in the open air, it must be protected from the rain.

Evaluation and testing. The Crescent stove costs little, is simple to build, is capable of bringing food rapidly to the boil, and

thereafter keeping it simmering for a long time. In addition, it offers a good degree of user comfort and is particularly recommended for single persons and small families. If maintenance and occasional minor repairs are properly carried out, this type of stove will give many years of service. The fuel-efficiency rate of the stove usually reads about 30%. Short water boiling tests (see section V) carried out under field conditions in Kenya during January 1983 indicated that 4.0 litres of water could be brought to the boil in about 13 minutes using on average 0.3 kg of wood as fuel (i.e. 75 g per litre of water boiled). Long water boiling tests showed that it was possible to bring 6.0 litres of water to the boil, and keep it boiling and simmering for a total of 60 minutes using 722 g of wood. Consumption was thus calculated at 120 g per litre per hour.

At a public demonstration, conducted during the International Conference of Non-Governmental Organisations on *Energy and Development* in Marseilles on 13th May 1982, 5.5 kg of rice and 9.5 kg of meat with sauce were cooked, using a Crescent stove in conjunction with a hay box, on 1.5 kg of wood. As the food was being served to a long line of guests the food was kept simmering for longer than would be necessary under strict test conditions. Despite this, however, the specific consumption of wood was recorded at 100 g per kg of food cooked.

The Pogbi or 'Ruthigiti' stove

History. This model was inspired by the **Nouna stove** which was developed, tested and promoted — first in Nouna and later in other parts of Upper Volta — by Rosemarie Kempers, a German volunteer nurse.

The Nouna, which corresponds to the needs and preferences of local women, is built with bricks or hollow cement blocks held together by mortar. It is covered with a **reinforced concrete** heating plate with openings to accommodate two pots.

The Pogbi retains the dimensions of the Nouna but is constructed out of clay. In addition the heating plates are made from **cast iron** or **sheet metal**. There is an arrangement for pre-heating secondary air, a fire-box ensuring optimal combustion and the provision of a whirl, or vortex, of gases around the pots. These improvements result in increased fuel efficiency and, if properly constructed, the Pogbi[22] is more durable than the Nouna model. In Kenya, the Pogbi is known as the *Ruthigiti stove*, after the name of the village where a number have been built and tested since 1981. The stove functions well on wood waste or combustible rural waste, and is part of a cooking system which includes cooking pots that enter deep into the fire-box.

The Pogbi is currently being used in Kenya, Pakistan and Switzerland. Results to date have been satisfactory.

Description. The body of the stove is constructed out of clay, either on site or in a local workshop. The designs are given in Figures 21 to 29. It is covered with a metal

Figure 21 *Pogbi stove — general view.*

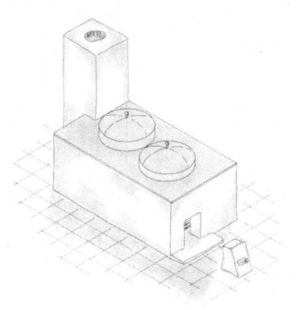

Figure 22 — *Moulds for making the Pogbi.*

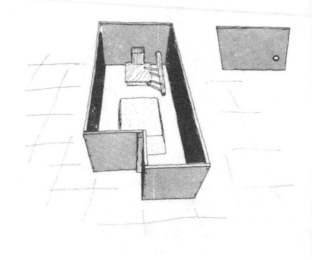

A Pogbi stove in a Kenyan village.

22. In the Mossi language the word *Pogbi* signifies a nice, young lady. It was suggested by Voltaic ladies working with Miss Kempers.

38

Figure 23 *Side-section.*

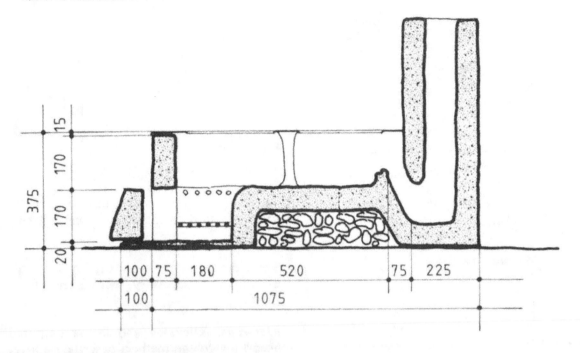

Figure 24 *Cross-section.*

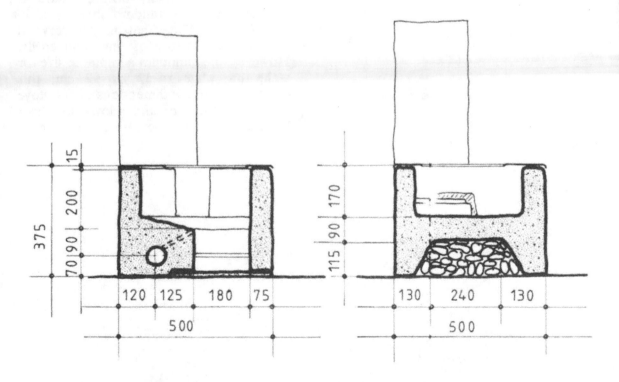

39

Figure 25 *Top view.*

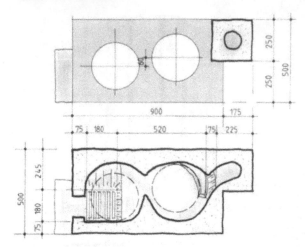

Figure 26 *Front view.*

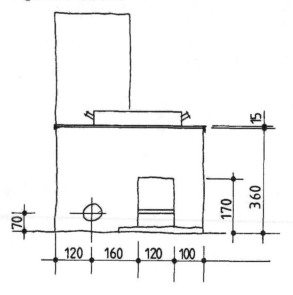

Figure 28 *Cross-sections with pots.*

Figure 27 *Side-section with pots.*

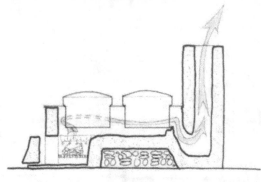

heating plate, equipped with two openings to accommodate more than one cooking pot.

The chimney is made out of clay segments extended, if necessary, with sheet metal pipes.

Materials. The clay should be prepared according to the method described above. The heating plates should ideally be made from cast iron, but if this is not available metal sheet, with a thickness of 1.5 mm, is a satisfactory alternative. Care should be taken to cut as many heating plates as possible from the standard sheets sold in local markets. The offcuts may be recycled for the manufacture of rings and cowls. However, the minimum acceptable size for a heating plate is 52 by 92 cm; this corresponds to the dimensions of the stove top (50 × 90 cm) and allows sufficient leeway for a lip to be formed in order to

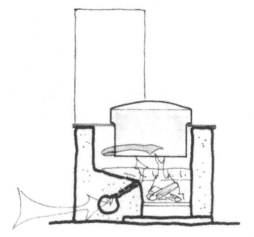

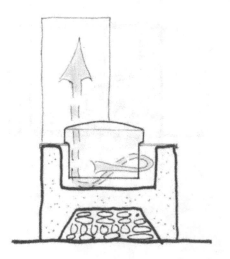

40

Figure 29 *Sheet-metal heating plate.*

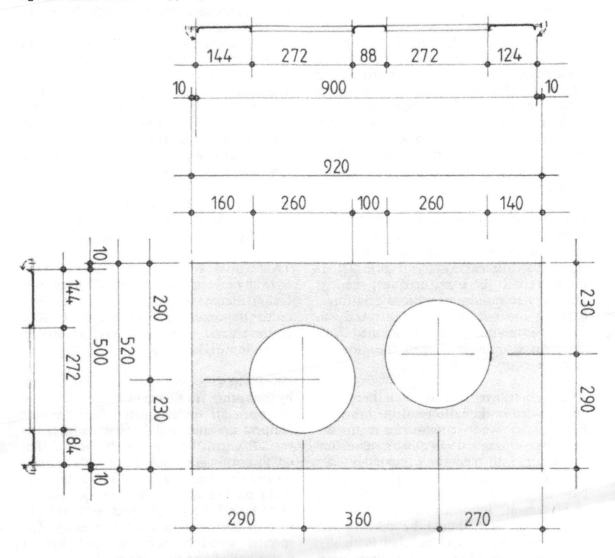

secure the heating plate firmly to the stove. As it is formed with a hammer this lip is curved slightly inwards and not bent exactly at right angles to the main surface of the heating plate. This increases its size by about 5 mm. For optimal security it is a good idea to rivet four metal sheet bands to the plate and to anchor them into the body of the stove when it is dry. This diminishes the danger of the plate warping.

As may be seen from the diagrams, the two pot openings are not cut exactly on the middle axis of the plate. Instead the centres of the openings are positioned respectively 3 cm to the left and right of the mid line

(see Figure 29). At first, the openings should be made sightly smaller than the diameter of the standardised pots. They are subsequently widened to the correct size with a hammer. This process causes a lip to be formed around the edges of the opening, thereby strengthening the plate and making it easier to insert and remove pots without scratching them.

The procedure described above may at first appear difficult. It should, however, cause few problems for experienced craftsmen. Indeed, during field work, selected Kenyan villagers and Afghan refugees became fully proficient in the construction of Pogbi stoves after only two to three weeks training.

Construction. The first step is to level the ground. Where necessary, a shallow foundation may be made with stones and gravel. The Pogbi is a low stove. However, it may be raised to the desired level by first building a stand with bricks or stones and clay. A good idea is to build a stand consisting of two parts, between which firewood and/or household effects may be stored.

Moulds, made out of metal sheets or other suitable materials, are used to ensure that the stove may be built rapidly, according to the correct dimensions (see Figure 22). If the stove is to be constructed on site it is necessary to build a provisional platform, between the two parts of the stand, on which the moulds may be positioned. This platform is removed when the stove is completely dry.

After a first layer of clay, 5 cm deep, has been placed in the bottom of the principal mould, the work commences with the **precise** positioning of all other moulds (for the door, ash chamber, secondary air ducts etc.) Some stones are placed at the base of the stove, below the second pot emplacement, in order to economise on clay. Great care should be taken when filling to ensure that the clay is tightly compacted around the moulds. Each lump of clay and hay mixture should be pressed around and along the contours of the stove to increase the strength of the structure. The clay should be well kneaded with the hands and fingers to avoid any air pockets.

Once the body has been moulded, the work may be completed by hand, provided always that the design is respected. However, once again, moulds may be usefully employed in the construction of the main combustion chamber, the emplacement for the second pot and the interconnecting gas passage. Similarly, the correct internal diameter of the chimney in the stove body may be obtained if a bottle or pipe is used as a makeshift mould. The entrance to the chimney should be of the same diameter as the chimney itself. This simple point is often overlooked by beginners in the art of stove making.

Great care should be taken to ensure that the heat is evenly distributed between the two pots. If the passage between the two chambers is too narrow it may result in too much heat being concentrated around the first pot, at the expense of the second.

Testing. Fuel consumption is low and cooking is both easy and comfortable. The heat absorption of the pots is good.

The Pogbi or Ruthigiti stove has now been tested by several stove experts. The average fuel-efficiency rate recorded is about 30% on the first opening and between 5 to 10% on the second, giving an overall reading in the region of 35 to 40%.

Short water boiling tests were carried out by the author, in Kenya in January 1983, in the open air under shelter. The ambient temperature and initial water temperature was 20°C to 23°C. The tests showed that 4.0 litres of water could be brought to boil, on the first opening, in 14 to 16 minutes, using on average 260 g of wood. At the same time 3.0 litres of water were brought to over 50°C on the second opening. The specific wood consumption per litre of water boiled was thus about 65 g.

Rotating three pots, each containing 6.0 litres of water, on the two openings it was possible to boil 24 litres in 58 minutes, using 1.5 kg of wood or 62 g per litre of water boiled. In addition a further 6.0 litres of water was brought to 81°C, and yet another 6.0 litres to 34°C. If these figures are converted into litres of water boiled a result of 50 to 55 g of wood per litre is obtained.

The fuel efficiency of stoves depends to a large measure on the way they are used.

In January and February 1983 the author

and Mr Haas controlled a sample selection of stoves produced and distributed during the previous year by the workshop established in Ruthigiti village. The stoves checked were being used daily to the owners' satisfaction and no complaints were recorded. This being said, none of the stoves were being operated in accordance with the instructions given. In particular:

— they were not being cleaned daily and, in many cases, the ash chambers were full of spent ashes
— the women usually kept the stove doors permanently open, and often the clay blocks designed to close the openings had been lost altogether
— the wood used was hardly ever cut into small pieces, and the stoves were invariably overcharged with fuel
— none of the stoves were being used in conjunction with hay boxes
— beans and dry maize grain were rarely soaked prior to cooking
— none of the users had swept the chimneys of their stoves.

Another view of the Pogbi stove.

Our criticisms were received with astonishment. After all, cooking on the new stoves was so much better and easier than before, so why bother with details! Obviously, it will require as much hard work to instil in the users the importance of **using** the stoves correctly, as in constructing them.

Peasant stove

History. The following three models — Peasant, Rural and Farmhouse stoves — are inspired by stoves that have been used in rural areas of Europe. The primary purpose in presenting them is to inform readers about the technical solutions, such as the pre-heating of primary and secondary air, the regulation of draught and the use of residual heat to heat water, which have been applied with success, and which could still be useful for the design of fuel-efficient stoves in developing countries.

The Peasant stove is made out of local clay. It is covered with a cast-iron or sheet metal heating plate. The stove should only be used with appropriate cooking pots. This again underlines the main theme of this book, namely that, as in the past, it is essential to use metal heating plates and matching cooking pots to achieve a truly efficient, fuel-saving stove.

Description. The main body of the stove consists of a block of clay built on the site. The designs are given in Figures 30 to 35. The fire-box has double walls but, in order to simplify construction and keep expenses to a minimum, there is no grate. Primary air is heated in the sheet metal door as described on page 10. Secondary air is admitted through two ducts and passes through the space between the two inner walls around the fire-box, where it is pre-heated before entering the stove.

Materials. The stove is made from clay, prepared according to the method described in section O. The heating plate is either made out of cast iron or, by local craftsmen, from metal sheet. The door is constructed out of recycled sheet metal.

Construction. The Peasant stove, like the Pogbi, is constructed with the aid of moulds. The first step is to level the ground and, if necessary, build a foundation with stones and gravel. Alternatively, the stove may be built on a twin pillar stand as described in the section dealing with the Pogbi. The basic mould consists of four boards, placed according to the dimensions of the stove. Two holes are made in the front board, through which two pieces of wood, 5 cm in diameter, are inserted to form the ducts for secondary air (Figure 33).

When the bottom of the mould has been filled with a layer of clay about 6 to 7 cm deep, additional moulds are positioned for the door as well as for the spaces between the inner walls of the fire-box and the body of the stove. The basic mould is then filled with clay to the top, and the combustion chamber is formed with the hands.

When the clay is half dry the moulds are removed and the heating plate is positioned on top of the semi-dry walls.

The chimney may either be fashioned with the hands or constructed with chimney segments, as described on page 13.

If the clay has been well prepared a **small** fire may be started in the stove a day or two after removal of the moulds in order to speed up the drying process. The stove may be used for cooking within about two to three days.

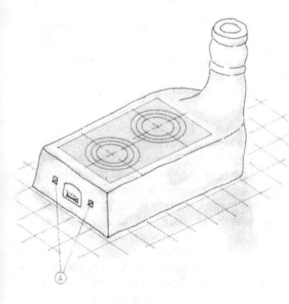

Figure 30 *General view of the Peasant stove.*

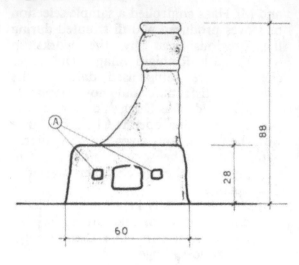

Figure 31 *Front view.*

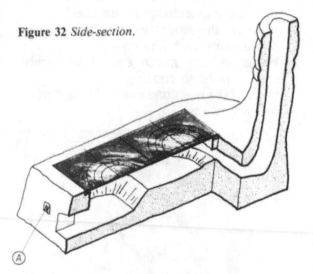

Figure 32 *Side-section.*

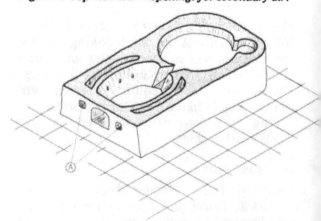

Figure 33 *Top view. A = openings for secondary air.*

Figure 34 *Top view of covered Peasant stove.*

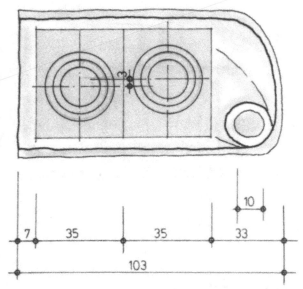

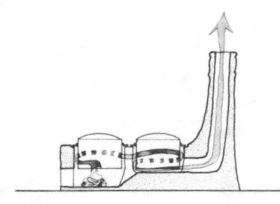

Figure 35 *Side-section with pots.*

Rural stove

History. The design of this stove was inspired by the small stoves that have always been popular in Europe, where they are also used for heating premises. On these models cooking is an ancillary function — which explains why they are often constructed out of cast iron plates that are conducive to heat radiation.

The Rural stove presented below has been designed specifically for cooking. **Its use should be limited to regions where there are no serious shortages of firewood.**

Description. The Rural stove is suitable for a small family, which does not need the facility of cooking with two pots at t same time. Optimal fuel efficiency achieved through:
—a carefully designed fire-box
—the provision of pre-heated primary and secondary air
—the use of a baffle to slow down the exit of gases
—regulation of air intake through the door.

To ensure proper functioning and maximum efficiency, **the use of a metal heating plate and standardised cooking pots is essential.**

Materials. Stones as well as baked or unbaked bricks may be used to construct Rural stoves. Once again, however, the best material is clay, prepared according to the method described in section O.

The grate may be manufactured from pieces of construction iron and the doors, plus the baffle covering the exit to the chimney, from recycled metal sheets.

As always, the main problem is the choice of material for the heating plate. Preferably, as was mentioned before, it should be made out of cast iron, but if this is not available sheet metal 1.5 mm thick constitutes a satisfactory alternative.

Construction. All the component parts of the stove should be prepared in advance.

If the body is made from clay, it may be constructed on site with the aid of moulds. For a competent stove maker, working with an assistant, this process will take up to two hours.

After the external moulds have been removed, iron rods or sticks, with a diameter of 8.0 mm, are used to make two holes on each side of the stove. These holes, which will allow for a supply of secondary air, should be directed **downwards**. In this way, the volume of air entering the stove will be automatically diminished as combustion slows down.

The principal disadvantage of this type of stove catering for only one pot is that it is difficult to avoid an undue loss of heat through the chimney.

To alleviate this shortcoming, a sheet metal baffle is placed on a platform built under the entrance to the chimney. This prevents gases from leaving the stove by the direct route, and forces them to exit via narrow passages above, and on both sides of, the baffle.

A movable plate — or **damper** — which is used to regulate the draught, is placed at the entrance to the right-hand passage. At first, this passage is left completely un-obstructed, but is gradually narrowed by the damper as combustion proceeds.

Figure 36 *A side view of a Rural stove. A = openings for secondary air.*

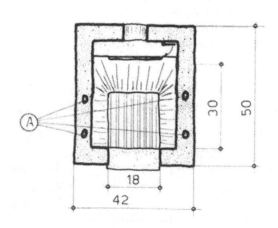

Figure 37 *Top view.*

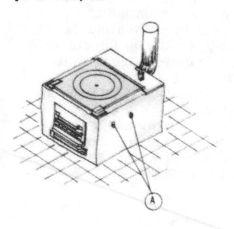

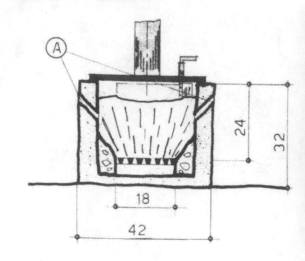

Figure 38 *Cross-section.*

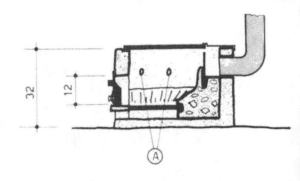

Figure 39 *Side-section.*

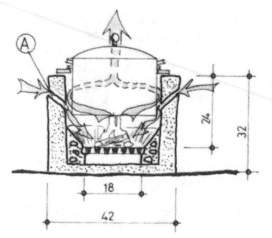

Figure 40 *Cross-section with a pot.*

46

Figure 41 *Side-section with a pot (Rural stove).*

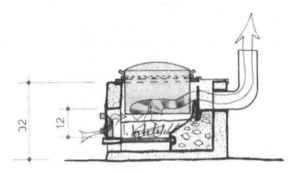

Farmhouse stove

History. The design is based on traditional European stoves used for large families as well as for small communities such as schools and dispensaries.

Description. The Farmhouse differs from the Rural stove in that it has **two** openings equipped with rings to accommodate different sizes of pot (see Figures 42 to 45).

A third emplacement is not provided as long experience has shown that the heat which may be recuperated around a third pot is not sufficient for the cooking of meals.

This surplus heat is not, however, wasted in the Farmhouse stove. It is used to heat water, for domestic use, in a tank situated at the rear of the stove.

The fire-box is fashioned according to the principles outlined on page 8 and repeated in the description of the Pogbi stove.

The door and the grid may be placed in the middle of the stove, but it is preferable to position them slightly to the right in order to maintain the flames for as long as possible around the base of the first pot and to facilitate the vortex effect.

The design provides for a supply of primary and secondary air, both of which are pre-heated, the former by the door and the latter by openings in the stove walls.

As in the Rural stove, these openings are directed **downwards** so as to avoid the admission of excess air towards the end of combustion.

The stove is covered by one sheet metal or two cast-iron heating plates. The first pot emplacement is positioned slightly to the right of the centre and the second slightly to the left. This enhances the vortex effect and ensures a good heat current around each pot.

The most direct route by which gases may leave the stove is along the sides of the water container at the rear of the stove. However, a damper is placed in this direct path. At the beginning of combustion the passage is left open in order to increase draught, but as combustion proceeds the damper is closed **so as to direct the gases round the water container** — which is heated in the process.

The water container is designed so that it may be removed to allow easy access to the stove for cleaning and removing soot.

Figure 42 *A side view of a Farmhouse stove.*

Figure 43 *Top view.*

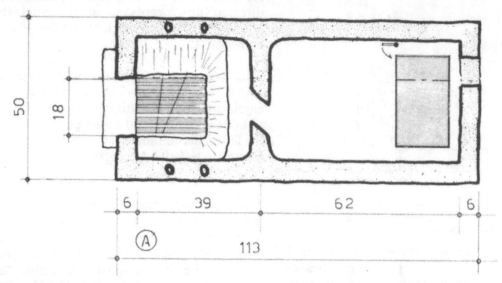

Figure 44 *Side-section.*

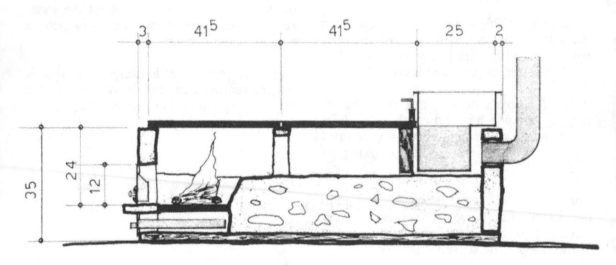

Materials. The basic materials are the same as those required for the construction of the Rural stove, namely baked or unbaked bricks, or clay mixed with hay.

Once again, it is essential to use efficient, standardised pots with the stove.

The water container may be fashioned out of mild steel sheets, at least 1.5 mm thick.

Construction. As with the Rural model, the quickest and most convenient means of constructing the stove is to use clay and moulds. This method ensures that all the

dimensions of the stove are respected.

If all the materials have been well prepared in advance, the stove may be constructed in a matter of hours. It will be ready for use two to four days later.

Testing. The stove gives complete satisfaction to its users. It boils food rapidly on the first pot and then allows for long simmering on the second. In addition, it supplies an ample volume of water which is hot enough for most domestic uses. The main shortcoming is that water is heated whether it is needed or not.

48

Figure 45 *Side-section with pots.*

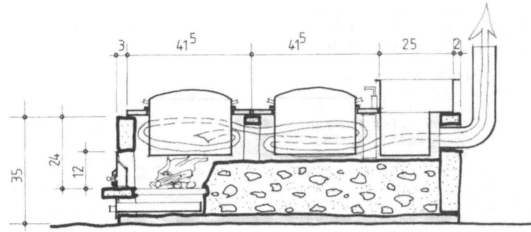

Q. Portable metal braziers

Polish stove

History. The name of this stove originates from the author's intention to design a simple stove, for small Polish farmers, to steam potatoes on combustible rural waste. The stove never arrived in Poland, but in time was developed as a brazier, working with wood or wood waste, to replace traditional charcoal stoves.

Often in developing countries city dwellers do not have separate kitchens. Thus, to avoid smoke in the living area stoves are ignited outside the house. They are only brought inside when combustion is well advanced and the smoke has diminished. Charcoal produces little smoke, which is one of the principal reasons for its popularity as a fuel for cooking.

The Polish stove offers the advantages of a charcoal brazier, but is far more efficient, more convenient, and runs well on more economical fuels such as wood, wood waste and other combustible waste. Towards the end of combustion, it produces as little smoke as a charcoal brazier.

The cooking procedure is the same as for a traditional metal brazier, namely the stove is lit outside the premises and brought inside when the food has boiled and the wood or other fuel has changed into glowing embers.

A large, specially designed cooking pot, which enters deeply into the stove, absorbs heat, saves fuel and contributes to ease of operation in the open air — even in unfavourable weather conditions.

Mr Emil Haas with a Polish stove.

49

Description. The stove takes the form of a cylinder, with double walls, welded to a round metal sheet base, and enclosed from above by a metal ring (see Figures 46 to 49).

An **inner structure** is then lowered inside the double walls. This consists of an open-cone fire-box, into which holes are drilled to allow for the admission of secondary air, and a metal cylinder which protrudes 10 mm above the outside walls of the stove. This arrangement provides for the entry of air, which passes between the body and the inner structure before entering the fire-box as pre-heated secondary air. When the ash-box door is closed part of the same air will serve as primary air, entering the fire-box from below the grate.

The ash tray is pulled out to light the fire, or during operation to increase draught.

Figure 46 *General view of the Polish stove.*

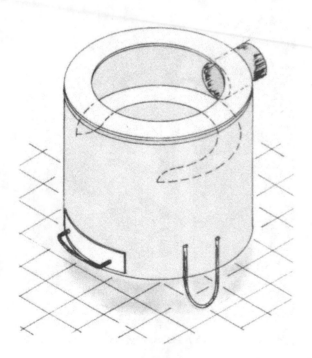

Figure 47 *Top view.*

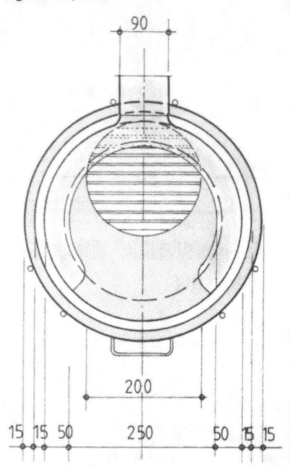

A crescent shaped platform — on which the cooking pot will stand — is welded to the inside walls of the inner structure. In the model shown here this is 3 cm above the line where the conical fire-box joins the upper cylinder.

In operation, the flames and gases first heat the base of the pot. They are prevented by the crescent platform from leaving the stove directly, and are forced to **flow around the sides of the pot** before departing via the chimney. In this way the heating surface of the pot is increased while the cooling surface is diminished.

The pot should only be filled to the level of the top of the stove in order to recover maximum heat. The rest of the volume of the pot compensates for a possible swelling of the contents.

Figure 48 *Cross-sections.*

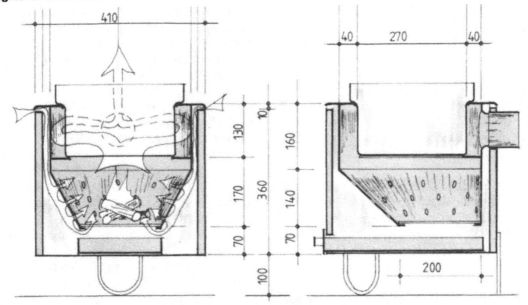

Figure 49. *Combustion chamber in the form of an irregular cone.*

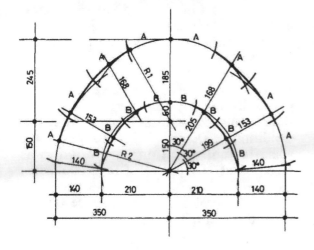

The volume of air entering from above is regulated automatically by the combustion process. Thus, when combustion is strong there is a correspondingly strong suction of air — which gradually diminishes as combustion slows down.

Materials. All parts of the stove are made out of mild steel sheets of varying thicknesses. The metal sheet for the crescent platform, which supports the pot and is subjected to high temperature, should be 2.0 mm thick. The same thickness should be used for the inner structure of the stove. The outside cylinders, which are not exposed to great heat, could conceivably be made from 0.8 to 1.0 mm grade sheet, which should be strong enough to support the cooking pot and withstand continuous transportation in and out of the house. This being said, however, 0.8 mm grade sheets are difficult to weld using acetylene. It is much more convenient to proceed by electric welding (where available) or even by simple rivetting. The choice of the most suitable technique must be left to the manufacturer concerned.

The Polish stove may be manufactured in any mechanical shop possessing welding facilities. The drawings used in this book should be adequate and comprehensive to an engineer. Detailed shop designs may, however, be necessary for the manufacture of the crescent platform and the fire-box cone.

The availability of metal sheet cutting and bending equipment would considerably increase labour productivity and diminish unit costs.

The experience gained during recent years

has indicated that the Polish stove presented in the first English edition was too small to meet the needs of the average African family. Another factor which influenced the decision to scale up the dimensions was that the use of larger pots would result in increased fuelwood economy. The new version presented here is for use with pots with a capacity of 8 to 9 litres, rather than 4 to 5 litres as was the case with the previous model.

Another design change has been in the form of the fire-box. In the new version of the stove, the fire-box is no longer a **regular** inverted cone. Instead, the shape has been rendered **irregular**, which makes it possible to prolong the flow of flames and hot gases under the pot, and thereby recuperate more heat. Cutting the form of the irregular cone may, of course, present problems. Engineers should experience little difficulty in reproducing the exact geometrical shape on the basis of the data given in the diagrams. However, non-qualified persons may find it more convenient to construct the cone by working from the simplified form given in Figure 49.

Once the form has been successfully reproduced, it should be preserved and used as a model for the construction of further stoves.

Evaluation and testing. A number of Polish stoves have been employed, in real working conditions, in West and East Africa, the Caribbean and in Europe. It has also been demonstrated on numerous occasions to groups of people interested in fuel-efficient stoves. The Polish stove has met with widespread support among users as cooking is fast, comfortable and very economical. Its manufacture presents no problems for professionals and may be carried out in any small mechanical shop possessing facilities for the cutting, rolling and welding of sheet metal.

The cost elements of the stove comprise approximately 15 kg of sheet metal, depending on the grade used, and two to three man/days' labour. The main obstacle to promotion is not so much technical as economic. In particular, the cost of sheet metal in developing countries is often excessive compared to ex-works prices in Europe, the United States or Asia. This renders the cost of the stove too high for the urban poor — even though in terms of fuel economy the investment may be recovered within a few months.

If, however, metal sheets could be made available at low cost the stove would stand an excellent chance of being adopted by local populations. As the fuel efficiency rate of the stove is up to 50%, considerable savings in firewood and charcoal could result if the stove were to be introduced on a wide scale. The stove may be run satisfactorily off a variety of fuels, including, notably, wood waste and other combustible waste. At a public demonstration during the 1982 International Conference at Marseilles cited earlier, 5.0 kg of rice and 9.0 kg of meat and vegetables were cooked, using a Polish stove in conjunction with a hay box, on 1.0 kg of wood.

As the food was being served to many guests it was kept simmering for longer than would be necessary under strict test conditions. Despite this, however, the specific consumption of wood was recorded at 71 g per kg of food cooked.

Among several tests, two may be quoted from those conducted in a Kenyan village in May-June 1982.

The first test took place in the open air, at mid-day with a slight breeze. The ambient temperature was 24°C; initial water temperature 22°C. Using 500 g of medium-quality wood 6.0 litres of water was brought to the boil in 14 minutes, and was kept boiling and simmering during the following 26 minutes.

In a subsequent test, under the same conditions, 4.5 kg of water was brought to the boil in 10 minutes. Then, 2.0 kg of maize flour was added and 6.5 kg of 'ugali' (a dense mash) was cooked in 20 minutes. The weight of wood was again 500 g. On this occasion the stove recorded a specific wood consumption of 77 g per kg of food cooked.

One disadvantage of the stove is that the pot must be removed to add additional fuel. The problem could be overcome by incorporating a door into the design, but this would have the drawback of increasing the production cost.

Nomad stove

History. The Nomad stove is the result of efforts to obtain a fuel efficiency similar to that achieved with the Polish stove. It was inspired, in particular, by the technology used in modern industrial and domestic boilers. It is specifically designed to meet

Figure 50 *A Nomad stove.*

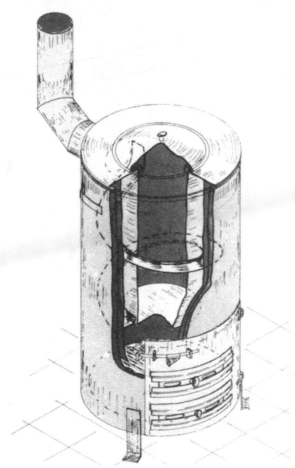

Figure 51 *Top view.*

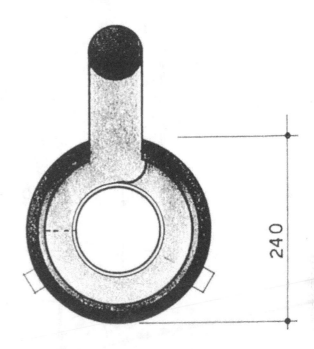

Figure 52 *Cross-section.*

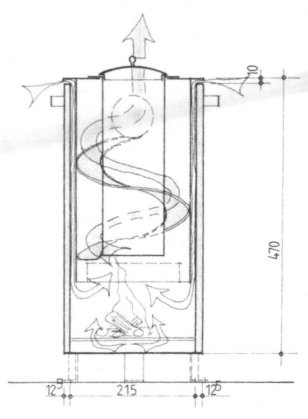

Figure 53 *Designs of stove elements.*

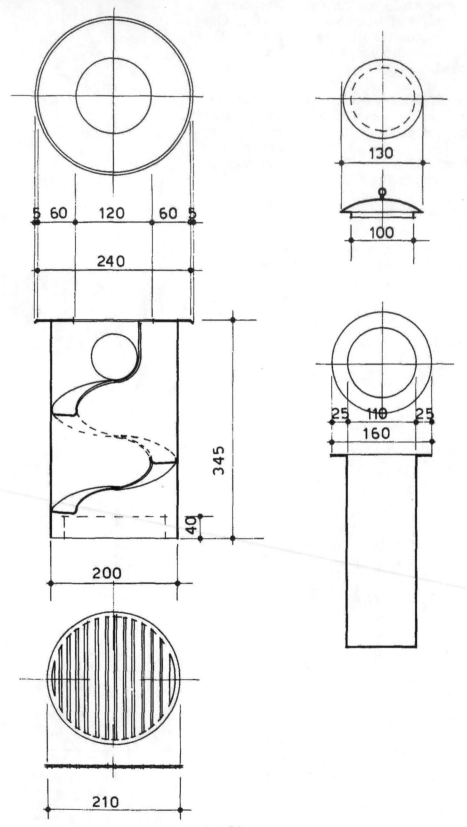

the requirements of those who need a stove to boil water rapidly, with the minimum possible fuel consumption. This is, for example, the case with nomadic communities living on the fringes of the Sahara region.

Description. Like the Polish stove, the Nomad has double cylindrical walls, welded to a circular metal base and closed from above by a metal ring. Another cylinder is placed inside the stove and protrudes 10 mm above the level of the external walls. A space of 30 mm is left between the double walls and the internal cylinder. This allows secondary air to enter from above, and be pre-heated before entering the fire-box.

A strip of metal sheet, 40 mm wide, is welded onto the inner walls of the internal cylinder. It takes the form of a spiral into which the cooking pot is placed. The innermost edges of the spiral (about 10 mm) are turned up to make a small wall. Holes about 5 to 7 mm in diameter, are drilled in the walls of the inner cylinder along the upper part of the spiral. Air, entering the stove from above, passes through these holes as pre-heated secondary air, which enhances the combustion of the gases flowing along the spiral.

The cooking pot has a capacity of 3.0 litres and an internal diameter of 110 mm. Its length, 300 mm, enables the gases to travel 1½ times round the pot as they proceed along the spiral.

The grate and the fire-box are situated in the lower part of the stove. The fuel is inserted through the door. Primary air may also enter through the openings made in the door.

Materials. The stove is made out of mild steel sheets. As with the Polish stove, the internal walls should be fairly thick as they are exposed to high temperatures. The external double walls may be shaped out of 0.8 to 1.0 mm sheets.

Construction. The stove, which appears somewhat complicated, is in fact probably easier to build than to describe! It does, however, require more skill and equipment than the Polish stove. The main construction problem is undoubtedly the cooking pot, which is the central feature of the stove.

Testing. The stove works well. For correct functioning little fuel should be used, and the pot should be filled with no more than 2.5 litres of water. These precautions prevent spillage caused by turbulent boiling.

The author and Mr M. Kinyanjui of Nairobi University discussing the design of a Nomad stove.

An open-air test was conducted in Switzerland in June 1981. The ambient air temperature was 16°C, and the initial temperature of the water in the pot was 10°C. There was a slight wind.

The fuel used was 0.25 kg of air-dried beech wood. 2.5 litres of water boiled, in an open pot, in 10 minutes, and continued to boil rapidly and simmer for a further 17 minutes.

Fuel efficiency, calculated according to the Eindhoven University formula (see page 86), was measured at 44%. It should, however, be recalled that this formula is based on the weight of water evaporated. With the Nomad stove the surface of evaporation is particularly small — which tends to lower the efficiency coefficient.

Figure 54 *A Family stove.*

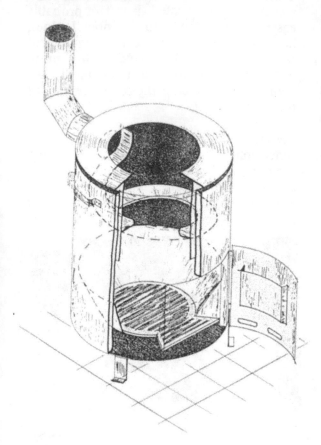

Family stove

History. This model represents an adaptation of the Nomad stove, designed not only to boil water but also to cook food. The volume of the pot is almost doubled, and the evaporating surface is quadrupled.

Description. The Family stove is a scaled up version of the Nomad model. The pot has a capacity of 7 litres and a length of 21 cm. All the other dimensions of the stove

Figure 56 *Cross-section and top view.*

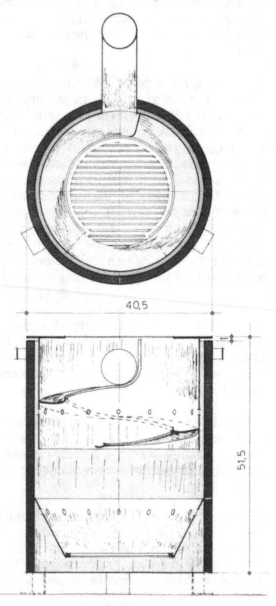

Figure 55 *Cross-section*.

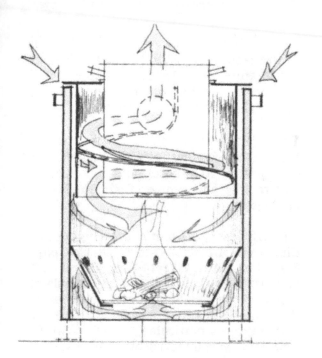

Figure 57 *Designs of stove elements.*

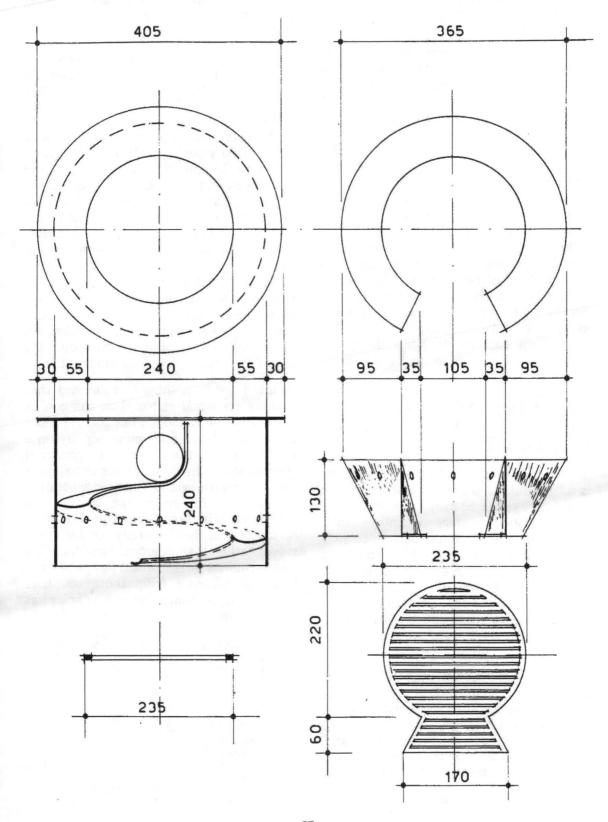

are increased proportionally from those of the Nomad. In the Family stove the gases flow once around the pot as they proceed along the spiral.

Testing. Tests were conducted under the same conditions as those described for the Nomad model. The following results were obtained: weight of water 4.0 kg; water evaporated 0.92 kg; wood used 0.5 kg. The water boiled in 10 minutes and continued to boil rapidly, and then simmer, for a further 18 minutes. Fuel efficiency, calculated according to the Eindhoven formula, was measured at 49%. This figure is higher than that recorded for the Nomad stove. The difference, however, is due to the **pot** rather than to the stove. Both stoves were tested under the same climatic conditions and with the same fuel. The higher efficiency coefficient recorded by the Family model points to the importance and usefulness of larger pots. The stove has often been successfully adapted, by the insertion of a burner, to run off biogas.

R. The use of charcoal

The burning of charcoal as fuel for cooking is a wasteful use of energy and should not be encouraged, especially in regions where the firewood shortage is most acute. Indeed, measures should be immediately introduced to progressively diminish the production and consumption of charcoal. These should include the introduction of efficient kilns and the promotion of fuel-saving stoves which burn wood-waste (and other combustible waste) rather than charcoal.

In developing countries, charcoal is produced in simple earth-covered kilns which do not capture any gases or liquid by-products. Due to the low efficiency of these kilns, as much as 8 tonnes of air-dried firewood (and sometimes more) is required to produce one tonne of charcoal.[23]

It follows that it is possible to extract four

to five times more heat from any given volume of firewood if, instead of being transformed into charcoal, it is burnt **directly** as fuel.[24]

However, the use of charcoal for cooking is a habit that is deeply rooted among certain communities, which understandably prefer to adhere to their ancestral methods. In addition, there are socio-economic factors to be taken into account as commercial arrangements dealing with the production and distribution of charcoal are well established and provide a source of income for a great many people. Also, in exceptional circumstances, the production of charcoal may be justified as it makes constructive use of wood waste that would otherwise be squandered. For these reasons, it is important not to abandon entirely research into stoves that allow more efficient use of charcoal. At the same time, however, steps must be taken to discourage, and gradually phase out, the use of this wasteful and outmoded fuel.

In this respect, it should be stressed that cooking on wood rather than charcoal is not only more economic but also far more convenient. Food boils more rapidly on a wood stove than on its charcoal counterpart. Also it is far easier to ignite the fire and to regulate the heat generated. If people are given the chance to experiment with both types of fuel, there is no doubt that they generally opt for wood stoves rather than charcoal braziers. This statement may be confirmed on the basis of historical evidence from those countries where the opportunity for such a choice has already arisen.

23. Thus, assuming that, on average, 8 tonnes of air-dried wood are needed to produce one tonne of charcoal, 1 kg of air-dried wood would yield only 0.125 kg of charcoal.

24. Potential heat of charcoal =

$$\frac{\text{Potential heat of wood}}{} $$

$$\frac{0.25 \text{ kg} \times 30,000 \times 100}{1.0 \text{ kg} \times 16,000} = 23.4\%$$

Assuming that:
— from 1.0 kg of air-dried wood one obtains 0.125 kg of charcoal
— the heat value of charcoal is 30,000 kJ
— the heat value of air-dried wood is 16,000 kJ.

58

The Kenyan Jiko

History. The author commenced his research into charcoal stoves early in 1979, at the request of senior officials from the Ministry of Energy and the National Council for Science and Technology in Kenya.

During the course of the following years several prototypes of improved charcoal braziers were built, used and tested in Switzerland and several developing countries.

In 1981, three models were selected for inclusion in the first English edition of this book. None of these have been retained in the present edition as subsequent research and field experience revealed that it was possible to achieve better results at lower cost with the new 'Kenyan Jiko' introduced below.

The brazier was designed to suit the characteristics of charcoal combustion but, at the same time, to promote the use of wood and wood waste for daily cooking.

Figure 58 *General view of the Kenyan Jiko.*

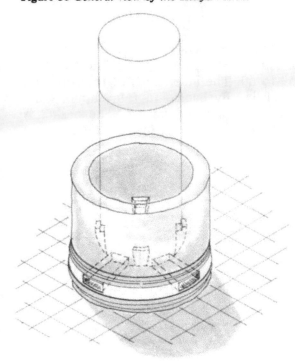

Figure 59 *Top view.*

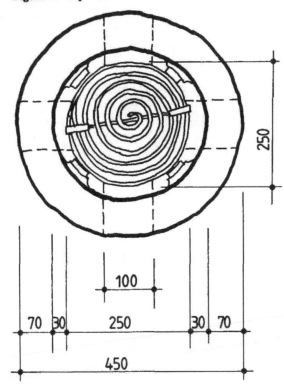

Care was also taken to keep the price of the brazier low and to ensure that it was simple to use.

One common problem with charcoal — particularly that smouldered out of dense wood — is that it is difficult to ignite. A considerable amount of air is needed for this purpose. Once the fire has been successfully lit, however, the volume of air must be reduced so as to prolong combustion. Thus, it was essential to incorporate into the stove design arrangements to meet these requirements.

Materials. On the basis of centuries of experience, clay is undoubtedly the most suitable material for the construction of charcoal braziers.[25]

25. Surprisingly, charcoal braziers made out of clay are rarely seen in African countries south of the Sahara where stove makers tend to employ recycled sheet metal for the purpose. In the Caribbean, people very ingeniously use discarded motor car wheels as bowls, with ready-made ventilation, for charcoal burning.

Figure 60 *Cross-sections.*

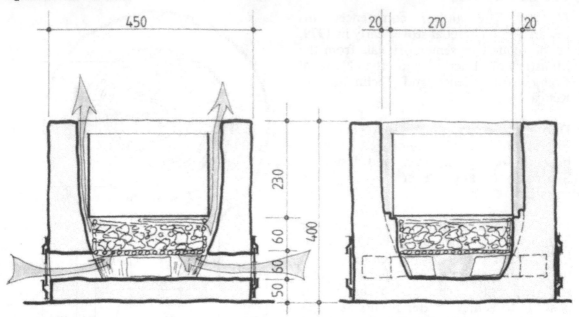

Figure 61 *Charcoal basket.*

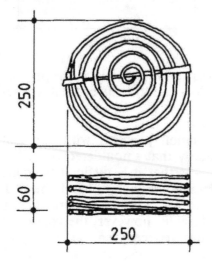

conical in form so as to facilitate removal when the stove has been completed). Next, four wooden boards, rounded at both ends to match the curves of the ash chamber mould and stove walls, are inserted to act as moulds for the air ducts.

In subsequent models, only three air ducts were made. This simplified the structure without diminishing the stove's efficiency.

The general design of the brazier is illustrated in the photograph and in Figures 59 to 60. The inner walls of the stove are modelled by hand and four supports are made for a metal basket. The basket is made from iron rods (diameter 7 to 8 cm)

Construction. The Kenyan Jiko is constructed with the aid of a cylindrical metal sheet mould, identical to that used to build the Protected Open Fire and Crescent stove.

The first step is to form the base of the stove by filling the cylindrical mould to a level of 5 cm. A cylindrical piece of wood, cut according to the dimensions given in Figure 59, is then placed in the middle of the stove to act as a mould for the ash chamber (the wood should be made slightly

Moulds for the Kenyan Jiko.

60

Set of moulds for the Kenyan Jiko.

and positioned just above the ash chamber. As there is space between the basket and the stove walls, air may enter it not only from below but also from all sides. On the stove walls at the upper level of the basket four ledges are cut on which the cooking pot will rest (in models having only three air ducts, of course, there will be only three ledges). The space between the outer surface of the pot and the inner walls of the

A Kenyan Jiko that has just been removed from the moulds.

stove should be about 2 cm, which is sufficient for the outgoing gases. With larger models it is possible to provide two sets of ledges, cut at different levels, so as to enable the stove to accommodate two different sizes of pot.

Operation. The stove provides a liberal inflow of air in order to facilitate ignition. Once the charcoal is glowing, however, a simple arrangement is provided to diminish the intake. This consists of a metal band which is placed around the outer walls of the stove at the height of the four (or the three) air ducts. The band has four (or three) holes cut in it which correspond with the openings of the air ducts. By rotating the band it is possible to close the openings, either partially or entirely, and thereby to regulate the supply of air to the stove.

The base of the pot stays on the basket and recuperates heat from the glowing charcoal. The sides are heated by the outflowing gases. As the walls of the stove are constructed from clay, heat loss through radiation is relatively low.

If the moulds, basket and clay are all prepared in advance the Kenyan Jiko may be constructed in about one hour. It is, thus, eminently suitable for local, small-scale production. However, before contemplating the introduction of this type of stove in a new region it is essential to determine the dimensions that would best suit the prevailing conditions and, in particular, allow the continued use of the most popular cooking pots available locally. In this context, users should, wherever possible, be encouraged to give preference to large pots which recover more heat. It may also be necessary to adjust the size of the air ducts to suit specific climatic conditions.

One of the most obvious shortcomings of the stove is its weight. Two people are needed to transport it even over relatively small distances. It may be possible to reduce the weight by making the stove shorter or by experimenting with thinner walls. Such improvements should not be overdone, however, as the stove must remain mechanically strong and provide good insulation for the heat generated by the burning charcoal.

The weight problem could, of course, be solved if the brazier were to be made with double metal sheet walls like the Polish stove described earlier. The air between the two cylinders would constitute an excellent insulating agent.[26]

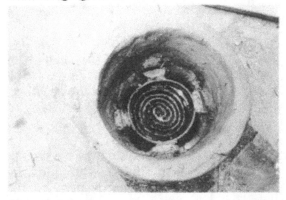

Internal view.

Testing and evaluation. It is far easier to ignite charcoal in the Kenyan Jiko than in traditional braziers. The fuel-efficiency rate is about 35 to 40%. This compares favourably with traditional metal sheet braziers, which usually give readings of between 20 and 25%. In addition, it is possible to regulate combustion, which saves fuel and makes cooking easier.

In one test 12.0 kg of water in two aluminium pots (each containing 6.0 kg) were boiled using 0.45 kg of charcoal. The specific consumption per litre of water was 34.6 g of charcoal. This result probably approaches the maximum that it is possible to obtain on rudimentary equipment under field conditions. However, it should be noted that, in terms of **wood** consumption, such a reading would correspond to only about 138 to 173 g of wood per litre of boiling water — a reading about two to three times inferior to the results obtained on the wood stoves described in this book. It should also be noted, of course, that the Kenyan Jiko may be fired — and will work well — with wood rather than charcoal.

S. Community stoves

History. Quite apart from normal family cooking, a great deal of firewood is used every day in the preparation of meals for the inmates of hospitals, dispensaries, children's centres, schools, army barracks, prisons and other public and private establishments.

Previously, such institutions often used butane gas in their kitchens. However, faced with serious procurement difficulties coupled with rising prices, many have been forced to revert to firewood.

This was the case, for example, with the Dagoretti Children's Centre, a home for disabled children located about 15 km northwest of Nairobi and administered by Cheshire Homes (Kenya), a charitable foundation.

The centre cares for about 150 disabled children, some of them bedridden. Meals were cooked outside the premises on open fires; consequently it was impossible to prepare hot food when there was rain or a strong wind.

In order to remedy this situation, the author, together with Mr Emil Haas, in January 1983 built at the centre the Community stoves described below.

Similar stoves, which can also be run off biogas produced on an installation designed by the author, were subsequently constructed at the 'Parking Boys' Centre; and at several schools, in Thika, Kenya.

In October of the same year another Community stove was built by Mr Haas and the author in the Nasr Bagh camp for Afghan refugees, near Peshawar in

26. At the time of printing, several prototypes of this type had been made and tested with good results. The designs and descriptions will be published in the specialized press and in future editions of this book.

Pakistan. This stove is operated mainly on bottled gas.

Description. Two versions of the Community stove are described in this section. Both are constructed according to the same principles and techniques. Only the dimensions differ. As can be seen from the drawings, the designs are based closely on those of the 'Polish' and 'Crescent' models. The first is a **universal** version equipped with a 42 litre pot for all-purpose cooking. The second has been specifically modified for the preparation of 'ugali', a dense maize mash which is the staple food of many Kenyan communities. Ugali has to be vigorously mixed and turned throughout the cooking process and the stove must, consequently, accommodate a sturdy, relatively shallow pot with a large diameter.

The Community stove should be constructed on a stone plinth. Its body is built with clay and the fire-box is lined with fire resistant bricks. The pot enters deep into the stove and rests on a platform built just above the fire-box. It is also supported by its rim which stays on the metal ring

Figure 62 *Universal Community stove — general view.*

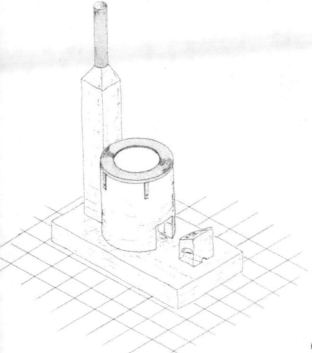

placed on the top of the structure. The fire heats the base of the pot and the hot gases flow over almost its entire surface (see Figures 62 to 64).

Materials. The basic materials used in the construction of the Community stove are local stones and clay mixed with hay, according to the method described on page 29 and below.

The clay selected should be suitably heat resistant, and it is a good idea to seek the advice of a local baked brick manufacturer on this matter. Alternatively, the brick manufacturer might be willing to sell pre-prepared clay. In this case, readers should wherever possible request clay destined for the manufacture of roof tiles.

As the fire-box is exposed to high temperatures it is advisable to line it with heat resistant bricks.[27] The stove would function satisfactorily without such a lining, but would require more careful maintenance and more frequent repairs.

The metal components for the stove are a cooking pot, ring, grid and stove pipe.

Construction. The first step is to level the ground and construct a plinth on which the stove will stand at the desired height. Sufficient space should be left on the front of the plinth to stand the large piece of clay which serves as a door and, at the rear, for the first chimney segment. It is also advisable to leave some space at the sides of the plinth so that users may use it as a step giving easy access to the stove for the purposes of raising and lowering the cooking pots.

The plinth may be built with any readily available materials such as stones, cement blocks or bricks. To economise on these

27. The bricks given in Figures 62 to 67 are 15 cm × 7 cm × 3 cm. If these dimensions do not correspond to the size of locally available bricks some improvisation will, of course, be necessary. It is important, however, when making adjustments to rigorously observe the basic design of the stove.

Figure 63 *Side-section*.

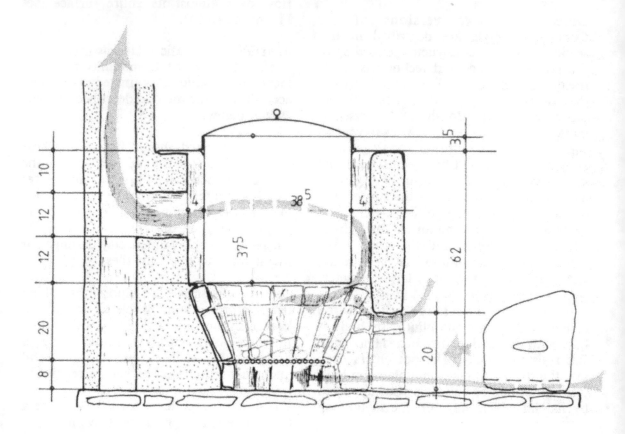

Figure 64 *Top view*.

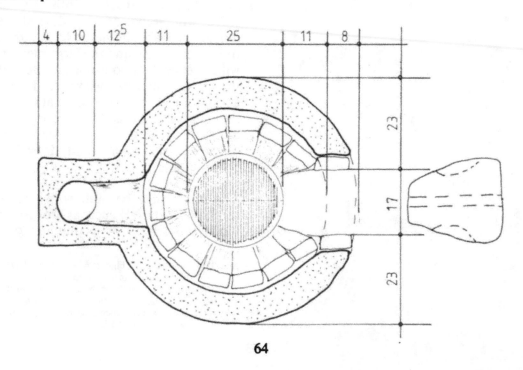

materials, the best pieces should be positioned on the outside edges of the plinth and, particularly, at the top. The inside of the plinth may be filled with rubble mixed with lumps of clay and hay.

Mr Emil Haas and an assistant cooking on Community stoves in Kenya.

Before commencing work on the body of the stove it is advisable to prepare a sheet metal mould of the correct height and diameter. This may be achieved by rolling the sheet metal into a cylinder and fastening it with two iron wires. The resulting **cylindrical mould** is then positioned on the plinth and filled, to a height of about 5 cm, with a first layer of clay mixed with hay. The cylindrical mould is then removed. The next step (see Figures 70 to 74) is to position a **rectangular mould** for the door and a **round mould** for the ash chamber. The door is reinforced on both sides with whole bricks and the ash chamber with half-bricks, positioned as shown in the diagrams. The base of the stove may now be filled with clay, taking care that the bricks and half-bricks remain in place and are firmly secured in clay. In this context, the bricks should first be watered so that the clay adheres to them well. In order to facilitate the operation, the filling process may be commenced without using the cylindrical mould. This should, however, be re-positioned as soon` as necessary. When the base of the stove has been filled with clay to the level of the top of the half-bricks, the next step is to start building the fire-box with clay —

taking care, as usual, to press the clay well in order to avoid air pockets. Once the basic shape has been formed, the fire-box may be lined with whole bricks. This is achieved by working up from the circle of half-bricks lining the ash-chamber. The first row of whole bricks will, thus, sit on the top of the half-bricks and be pressed obliquely into the clay walls of the fire-box. **Care should be taken to reserve a space of about 1.5 cm on the top of each half-brick so as to form a circular platform on which the grid will be placed. The use of a circular wooden mould may help meet this requirement.** When finished, the fire-box should be in the shape of an **open cone** conforming to the design specifications given in Figures 62 to 67.

Work on the fire-box is completed by placing a layer of half-bricks at the top of the lined structure so as to form a platform on which the cooking pot will rest.

Once the fire-box is completed the walls of the stove may be built up to the top. Again, to facilitate the work, as well as to render the walls of the stove more regular, one

Figure 65 *Community stove for Ugali (Tô).*

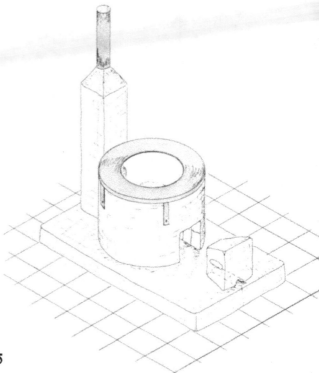

65

Figure 66 *Cross-section.*

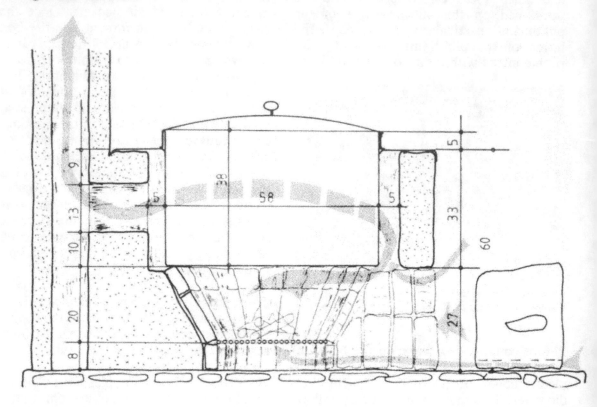

Figure 67 *Top view.*

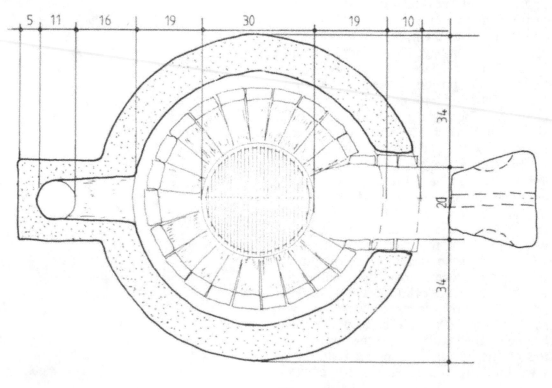

may use a **second metal cylindrical mould** which fits inside the first. The difference in diameter corresponds of course to the thickness of the stove wall, and it therefore suffices to fill the gap between the two moulds with tightly pressed clay.

About 10-12 cm above the platform, opposite the door, a rolled-metal tube, with a diameter of 12 or 13 cm (according to the type of stove built) is positioned as the mould for the chimney opening.

When building the wall it is important to allow for the propensity of clay to shrink, both laterally and vertically, during the drying process. Thus, the walls should be built about 3 cm higher and 1 cm thicker than indicated on the design drawings (which give the dimensions of a **dry** stove).

A small fire may be lit in the stove one day after completion, and it may be used for normal cooking two days later. **However, the drying process takes between 3 and 4 weeks, during which time regular adjustments should be made — particularly with respect to the height of the stove wall.**

As mentioned above, a **metal ring** covers the stove. Three metal bands are welded or rivetted to the ring so that it may be secured to the stove walls. Obviously, as the height of the latter is going to diminish during the drying process, the ring cannot be fixed definitively at the construction stage. However, **as soon as the stove is thoroughly dry** the ring may be permanently anchored to the stove by means of sturdy bolts which pass through the stove walls above the inner platform, and which are secured by nuts and large washers (made out of squares of metal band) on the other side. To provide further reinforcement the lower ends of the metal bands are bent at right angles to form lips, which can be hammered into the stove walls. **A piece of recycled metal sheet should be placed under each lip. This will keep the ring at a constant height and, should further shrinking occur, it would thus be possible to fill in the gap without removing the ring.**

Building and testing a Community stove in the Nasr Bagh camp for Afghan refugees, Pakistan.

The clay and brick work involved in making Community stoves presents no major difficulties for trained masons. Once all the necessary materials have been prepared and assembled one mason, working with two helpers, should be able to construct a plinth and stove within two days without undue effort.

Cooking pots and metal components. It has been a constant theme of this book that the optimal use of fuel is not possible without a complete cooking system which includes **properly designed pots**. This assertion is of special significance in the case of Community stoves, for the importance of the pots can be said to increase proportionally with the size of the stove. They must be well manufactured, preferably out of sheet steel as aluminium pots of the dimensions required may prove too weak. In addition, they must be capable of withstanding temperatures of between 500 and 800°C in the fire-box, as well as heavy food loads and rough daily handling. Pots used in the preparation of 'ugali' must be especially sturdy as the food must be beaten and turned with heavy wooden sticks during the cooking process.

For the models built at Dagoretti and Thika the author chose good quality **stainless steel** pots. Each was manufactured in three stages:

First, a cylinder was formed and welded out of 1.0 mm sheets of steel. Second, a circle was cut from another sheet of the same thickness[28] and welded to the cylinder in order to form the base of the pot. The ugali model was additionally reinforced by means of a second circular steel plate welded to the base.

The final stage was to fold back the upper edges of the cylinder in order to form an overhanging lip at the top of the pot. Part of this lip was then folded outwards at right angles so as to make the **rim** by which the pot stays on the metal ring covering the stove (see Figures 63 and 66). Two handles were then welded to the finished pot, just above the rim. Sheet metal tubes were placed around the handles in order to facilitate carrying as well as to protect the users' hands from the heat of the pot. Subsequently, in order to reduce the price even further, pots were manufactured from mild steel sheets and even improvised from diesel oil drums.

With the exception of the oil-drum models, the pots described above were manufactured in a well-equipped metalwork shop in Nairobi. The author recognises that similar facilities may not exist in other parts of the world and that some improvisation may be necessary in the light of local conditions. Thus in Peshawar, Pakistan in the autumn of 1983 a pot — of 74 l capacity — was manufactured out of copper sheets according to traditional technology. The parts of the pot were bent and hammered into the desired shape and then brazed together. The producer gave a five year guarantee for this vessel.

The pots should be equipped with properly designed lids. In particular, there should be a groove around the edges of the lid which fits over the walls of the pot. This arrangement ensures that condensed vapour is directed back **into** the pot rather than allowed to escape down the outside walls and on to the stove. Energy saving is also increased by the addition of such a groove.

The metal rings and grids did not present

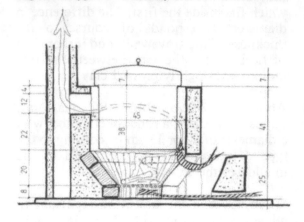

Figure 68 *Afghan community stove — cross-section.*

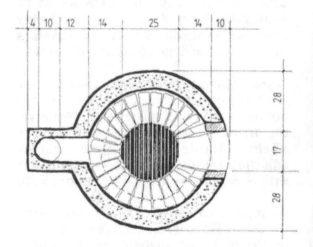

Figure 69 *Top view.*

any particular manufacturing difficulties. As can be seen from the diagrams, the width of the rings should be equal to that of the stove walls plus the space needed for hot gases to flow around the pots.

In order to withstand heavy loads and rough treatment the rings should be made from metal sheets of not less than 2.0 mm grade. For the 'ugali' model in particular it would be preferable to use 3.0 mm grade. Manufacturing such rings is too difficult for workmen equipped with only hammers and chisels, and the task should be entrusted to a properly equipped metal workshop.

28. Subsequent experience tended to indicate that, in order to render the pot used for *ugali* even more resistant to rough handling, it was advisable to cut the circular base from thicker steel.

A considerable safety margin was allowed in calculating the resistance of the stove walls, which are easily strong enough to support the weight of the pot and contents as well as to withstand rough handling.

For the construction of the chimney, the reader is referred to page 13.

Figures 70-73 *Stages of construction.*

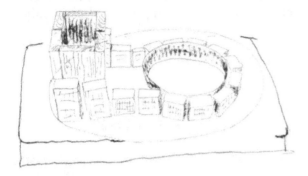

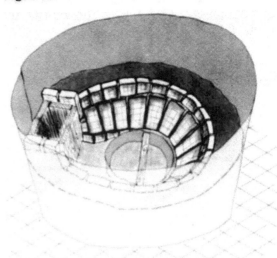
Figure 72.

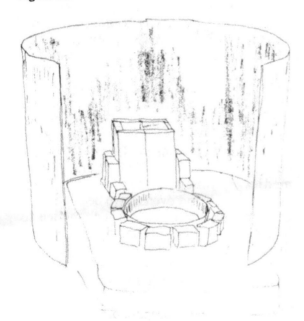

Figure 71.

It is not necessary to put more wood in the stove after the food has been brought to the boil. Instead, the stove door should be closed and a bag of hay placed over the covered pot. The stove now acts as a perfect hay-box (see page 25). Over two hours the temperature of the boiling food will only drop by about 2 to 4°C. During trials in the Dagoretti children's centre in Kenya the author established that, if the dry foodstuffs were pre-soaked and care was taken to maintain a proper fire, the consumption of firewood needed to cook a typical meal of beans and dry corn for the

Figure 73.

Testing and evaluation. The firewood economy achieved on the stoves was considerable. For example, the cooking time for dry beans was reduced from 4 to 5 hours to 15 to 30 minutes. This reduction in cooking time is also due to the fact that the beans were pre-soaked (see section on cooking methods on page 26).

centre could be reduced from the approximately 50 kg used previously to about 6 kg.

Figure 74 *Fire-box with a grid*.

The durability of these stoves will, of course, depend on proper use, care and maintenance. It is, for example, particularly important to avoid overheating and to protect the stoves, as far as possible, from water. In addition they should be cleaned daily and regularly inspected for signs of damage to the clay and brickwork — both inside and outside. Should any deterioration be detected, the used clay should be removed from the areas in need of repair (when the stove is completely cold) and replaced with new clay mixed with hay.

From time to time, it is essential to check the clay joints between the bricks. In order to render these more durable and reduce the need for repair stove makers may prefer to use heat resistant cement for these joints. It is stressed, however, that good quality clay should prove quite satisfactory for normal use.

The problems and pitfalls confronting the makers of efficient stoves are magnified as the size of the model increases. With Community stoves it is more than ever essential to pay careful attention to the guidelines and basic principles outlined earlier in this book. Given adequate designs, the construction of fuel-efficient stoves is a relatively easy task. However, their proper use, repair and maintenance is more complex and may only be learned properly through experience. Until more attention is given to training local craftsmen and teaching these skills widely among the users it will be difficult to achieve the desired and possible levels of firewood economy.

T. Bread ovens

The problem of bread baking has been studied in various parts of the world for many centuries. There exists ample documentation on the subject containing ideas which may readily be adapted to the conditions currently prevailing in developing countries.

Throughout the ages, humanity has evolved a considerable number of ovens and baking techniques — from the most rudimentary to the more sophisticated methods which came to Europe with the Greek and Roman civilisations. From medieval times onwards, countless examples of bread ovens have been made in Europe. Many still consider such models to be among the finest invented and, indeed, there is currently a tendency towards their revival by those disillusioned with the bread produced on modern industrial equipment.

It is not possible to prepare bread on flames or embers. It must be baked using *accumulated heat*, usually stored in stones, bricks or clay, which must be evenly distributed over all sides of the dough.

If the latter principle is not observed, one side of the loaf will come out of the oven charred while the other side will be unbaked. This is not only a matter of taste but also a health hazard, as bread prepared in this way may often be the cause of digestive ailments.

In order to achieve fuel economies in the baking process, people progressively abandoned small, individual stoves in favour of larger bread ovens. These could either be shared by several families or run by village bakers working for a number of consumers. Such installations were a common sight in European villages until fairly recent times and they were used on a continuous basis by the inhabitants. The principal advantage of such ovens was that, once they had been brought to the correct temperature, only small additions of fuel were necessary to maintain the desired heat level over long periods.

To achieve optimum fuel economy, the oven should be well-insulated and opened as little as possible during use. It is thus a good idea to encourage, wherever possible, the baking of larger loaves. This consideration led, in Europe, to the gradual abandoning of small breads.

It should never be forgotten, however, that the baking of bread will always require a higher fuel consumption than the cooking of other foods, due to the need to build up accumulated heat. In view of this, it may be advisable in those regions most acutely affected by fuelwood shortages to encourage the consumption of cereals in forms other than bread (porridges, gruels, soups etc.).

For example, flour cakes or flat bread may be prepared in covered frying pans on the stove models presented in previous chapters. If the dough is correctly prepared and the frying pans well conceived, such cakes provide an economical substitute for bread baked in fuel-intensive ovens.

There are, however, numerous situations where the baking of bread is justified and necessary. This may be the case, for instance, when catering for hospitals, dispensaries, schools, orphanages or disabled children's homes where bread is badly needed. It may also be the case with large-scale public works, where hundreds of workers must be nourished every day, or with suburban settlements where good bread is often the best solution for basic daily nourishment.

For all the above situations, the author proposes the bread oven described in this chapter. It is relatively easy to construct and its efficiency is based on centuries of experience.

Making a mould for a bread oven in Nasr Bagh.

Construction of the bread oven

The construction method described below is based on the investigations and long experience of Pierre Delacrétaz, whose name has already been mentioned in this book in connection with the preparation of clay. Mr Delacrétaz has been passionately interested in bread ovens and the baking of bread for many years and is the current Chairman of 'L'Association pour la maison du blé et du pain' in Echallens near Lausanne. For a better understanding of the construction and functioning of bread ovens, readers are referred to Mr Delacrétaz's book, *Les Vieux Fours à Pain*, which has already been cited.

At the end of 1983, Mr Delacrétaz joined the author for a mission in the North West Frontier Province of Pakistan, where he introduced new models of bread ovens for use in Afghan refugee camps.

Bread ovens should be situated in bakeries with facilities for storing flour and preparing dough. The oven or ovens heat the bakery and ensure the steady temperature necessary for the primary and secondary fermentation of the dough prior to baking. The building of bread ovens is only part of the task; what really matters is the production of good bread. It is, therefore, strongly recommended to discuss matters with experienced local bakers *before* embarking on construction. Bakers usually recommend building two ovens in one bakery; this facilitates work, increases the productivity of labour and diminishes fuel consumption.

When the premises are already in existence, but there is no room inside for an oven (or where there is a need to economise space), the body of the oven may be constructed *outside* the building. It should, however, be protected from the rain under an extension roof. Only the face of the oven, with its opening and an arrangement for the evacuation of gases, need remain inside the premises.

It is, of course, possible to construct a bread oven which is not housed in a building but merely sheltered against the rain. If properly insulated, such an oven will function well, but users will face problems with the transportation of dough etc.

Figures 75-81 *Stages of construction of the bread oven.*

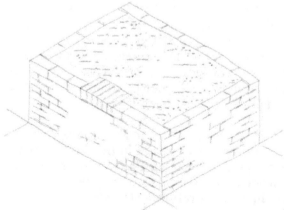

Work on an oven starts with the levelling of the ground and the construction of a plinth — the height of which should be about 70 cm, which makes it easy to maintain the fire, clean the floor and insert the loaves. The surface of the plinth should be larger than the base of the oven and should be covered with a layer of sand and silt up to 20 cm thick which serves as additional insulation.

The plinth consists of four walls constructed out of whatever material is available, for example stones or ordinary bricks. The space inside the walls is filled with well-packed earth, stones and sand. It is a good idea to build a niche on the front side of the plinth where one may keep a metal box to collect embers and ash from the oven, or stock firewood. The top of the plinth is covered with a layer of sand and a layer of clay prepared in the same way as the clay for the stoves described in previous chapters. The layer of clay, which serves as the floor of the oven, should be about 90 cm above ground level.

The floor is a vulnerable part of the stove as it must withstand constant shocks due to the pushing of fuel into different parts of the oven, the raking out of embers and the charging and removal of loaves. It is therefore advisable, whenever possible, to build the floor with fire-resistant bricks. In the absence of these, the clay floor should be treated with care and occasionally repaired. It is strongly recommended to incorporate into the clay floor a flat stone or fire-resistant brick at the entrance to the oven, which is the area most exposed to wear.

As soon as the floor is ready, the inner diameter of the oven must be established. For family ovens it may be fixed at 60-70 cm. For community use it may be increased up to 140 cm. The model described here will not function properly with a diameter larger than 150 cm. It should be noted, however, that an internal diameter of 140 cm gives a floor surface of 1.5 m² on which 40 loaves may be baked.

Naturally, it is possible to build much larger bread ovens, with internal diameters of 4.0 m or more, but a different design is required. In particular, the design must allow for the additional evacuation of gases from the *rear* of the oven in order to secure sufficient draught for the burning of increased quantities of fuel. Experience shows that exceptionally skilled bakers are also required for the operation of such large ovens.

Once established, the chosen diameter is marked on the plinth with the aid of a piece of string and chalk as a makeshift compass. An edge wall is then formed around the outside perimeter of the chalk marking. This should be made 20 cm thick and 20 cm high using well prepared clay mixed with long strands of hay (see section O). The completed wall forms the base of the vault. At the front of the structure, a curved band (15 cm wide) of sheet metal is positioned to form the arch over the future opening of the bread oven (see Figures 76 and 77).

Figure 76.

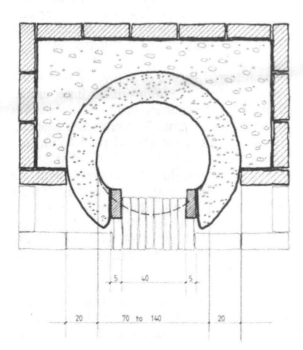

Figure 77.

Bands of plastic film (20-30 cm wide) are now positioned along the edge walls to maintain the mould around which the vault will be formed. The bands should be sufficiently long to cover the completed mould.

The mould is formed with bricks or stones criss-crossed so as to obtain the necessary volume with relatively little material and to facilitate the removal of the mould through the oven door when the finished vault is half dry. The bricks and stones are strengthened with clay and wet sand and the mould is formed with the hands and trowels. When completed, the mould is completely covered with the plastic film bands. To maintain the mould steady, the bands are positioned slightly crosswise. The ends of the bands are then trimmed where necessary so as to ensure that the outside surface of the mould is as smooth as possible. The dimensions of the mould (and by extension those of the vault built round it) are of the utmost importance in ensuring the efficient functioning of the oven.

There is no chimney built into the oven. When the fire is lit, air enters through the *lower* half of the opening. Glowing embers heat the floor and the flames and hot gases strike the vault before being directed, by the curved surface, out of the oven through the *upper* part of the opening. As bakers say, the fire must 'turn' in the oven.

Mr Pierre Delacrétaz examining a mould ready to be covered with plastic strips.

Figure 78.

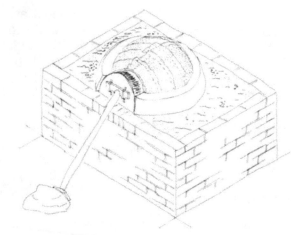

The inner proportions of the oven are crucial for good combustion, heat recovery and evacuation of gases. If the vault is too high and the opening too low, it will be difficult to achieve good combustion. On the other hand, if the opening is too high and the vault too low, heat recuperation will tend to be poor. After carefully measuring the proportions of a great many old bread ovens, Mr Delacrétaz established the optimal proportion of the inner height of the vault to that of the opening at 100 to 63. The author consequently ordered a family oven from an old Italian master, giving him *carte blanche* as far as the construction was concerned. Upon delivery, he found that the 100 to 63 ratio had been respected! It appears that the *width* of the opening is of less importance and should be decided by reference to ease

of operation and the size of the foods that the oven will be called upon to bake. For example, some stoves may occasionally be called upon to cook an entire lamb as well as bread!

Figure 79.

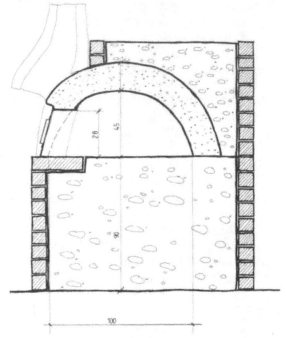

Once the principal mould is ready, the dome structure may be built around it. To strengthen the opening, bricks or stones may be positioned around the metal arch mould placed previously (Figure 79).

The internal height of the vault should be 10% less than the radius of the inner circle. For example, if the inner diameter chosen is 145 cm (i.e. radius 72.5 cm), the internal height of the vault should read 65 cm (or more precisely 65.25 cm). If the diameter is 80 cm, the height of the vault will be 36 cm. The resulting structure thus resembles a slightly flattened hemisphere. As mentioned above, the ratio between the inner height of the vault and the middle height of the opening should, in all cases, be 100 to 63.

A sheet metal door (2 to 3 mm thick) is used to close the opening. It is placed slightly obliquely and closes the opening by its own weight.

The construction of the oven is greatly facilitated if the door (or a board substitute of the same dimension) is held firmly in position with props from the outset of work. The hemisphere will be flattened not only at the top of the structure but also over the opening.

Figure 80.

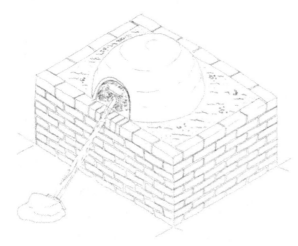

Building the dome does not present any particular difficulties. The lumps of clay used should be mixed with fairly long strands of hay and thoroughly kneaded to avoid air pockets. The final thickness of the walls should be about 20 cm (Figure 79).

Figure 81.

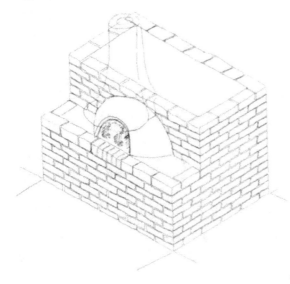

The bread oven in Nasr Bagh after removal of the mould.

Around the opening, a rim should be formed with clay in order to strengthen the structure and maintain heat close to the opening. If the oven is built in enclosed premises, it is important to form a smoke collector (built from clay or sheet metal) over the rim. The smoke collector will, of course, be linked to a suitable chimney (Figure 81).

As soon as the structure is half dry, the main mould may be removed piece by piece through the oven entrance. The plastic bands are also removed for possible future use. The inner walls and floor of the oven are then smoothed by hand or with a trowel. During the first three or four days of the drying process, a solution of salt and a little water should be rubbed daily into the inner walls of the stove. The salt penetrates the clay and, when subjected to heat, vitrifies to make the inner surface hard and smooth.

Some cracks are bound to appear during the drying process, particularly if the clay used was too wet. These may be repaired with clay held in reserve. The cracks should first be moistened with a little water and then well filled.

As soon as the structure is thoroughly dry (which may take up to two weeks), walls should be built around the plinth and the dome covered with a layer of sand and silt about 40 cm thick. This ensures that the oven is well insulated and keeps heat loss to a minimum.

The work of the oven builder thus comes to an end and that of the baker commences. Experienced bakers know exactly how to use ovens to their maximum capacity. They bake tarts, bread, rolls and pizzas. In addition, they roast meat and use the accumulated heat to dry fruit and vegetables. The remaining heat serves to dry firewood. Hardly any is wasted!

A bread oven running off bottled gas in the camp for Afghan refugees at Katcha Garhi, Pakistan.

U. Home heating devices

In a number of developing countries, even those situated in warm climates, the nights become decidedly chilly in some parts of the year, and in some cases (such as in Lesotho, Nepal and Afganistan) there are very cold days and frosty nights. Thus, the heating of premises is not merely a matter of comfort but one of survival.

The heating of premises demands the use of stoves equipped with chimneys such as the Crescent or Pogbi (the use of chimneyless stoves in the home should not in any event be encouraged as there is a serious risk of fatal intoxication).

In order to derive maximum benefit from the stoves one should use sheet metal chimney-pipes. During the winter a heat exchanger may be inserted into the lower end of the pipe. This device increases the heating surface of the chimney and represents a simple but efficient means of heating premises. Heat exchangers are widely used in Europe and are readily available on the market. When not required, the heat exchanger is simply removed and replaced with a conventional chimney section.

The manufacture of heat exchangers poses no particular problems and, given an adequate supply of the necessary sheet metal, they could even be produced in the villages where they are most needed. A better solution would be mass production of standardised exchangers in well equipped metal workshops.

Should the use of heat exchangers fail to provide a satisfactory solution, one may envisage the manufacturing of simple hot air generators. The models described below were designed by Mr Emil Haas for Afghan refugees in western Pakistan, where the nights can be very cold.

The first (Figures 82, 83) consists of a sheet metal cylinder closed at both ends. A metal pipe is inserted through the middle of this to form a cylinder within a cylinder (the end of the pipe protrudes from the top and bottom of the large cylinder). The heat source — which may, for example, be a wood stove, gas or kerosene burner — is placed at the base of the large cylinder.

Figures 82-83 *The cylindrical home heating device showing flow of hot air.*

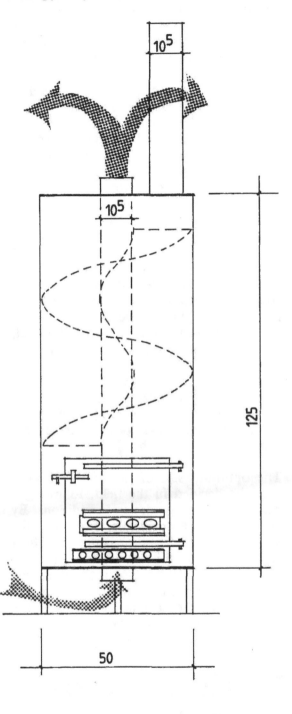

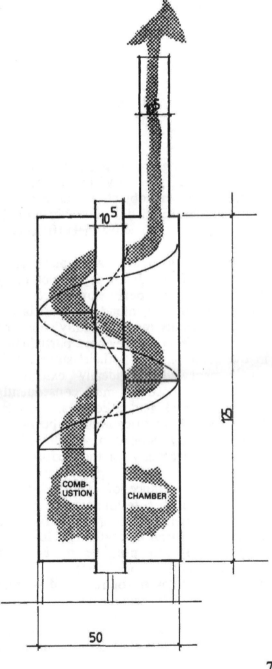

COMB-USTION

CHAMBER

Above the heat source an internal spiral is built in the space separating the two cylinders. The spiral twists through three turns and leads to a chimney which goes outside the premises.

77

In use, the hot gases heat the walls of the larger cylinder which warms the premises through radiation. Simultaneously, the inner pipe becomes hot so that ambient air entering the pipe from below is warmed and evacuated into the room from above.

This type of home heater was presented on the Bellerive Foundation's stand at the *Energy 83* exhibition held in Montreux in November 1983. The heat source used was a kerosene wick stove, distributed in large numbers by the Office of the United Nations High Commissioner for Refugees (UNHCR) among the Afghan refugees. The heater was found to perform very satisfactorily.

Another type of home heating device is presented in Figures 84 and 85. It is conceived according to the same basic principles as the model described above but is square in shape rather than cylindrical. In order to increase heating capacity, four inner pipes are incorporated into the device. The square shape makes the device easier to manufacture than the cylindrical version which may (especially with regard to the internal spiral) pose problems for inexperienced tinsmiths.

The optimum size of the heating devices must be decided in the field, following a period of testing under real conditions. By way of general principle, however, the larger the model the better its heat recuperation. In this respect height is more important than the surface of the base. Due consideration must also be given to the size of the average home to be heated and to the limited purchasing power of the users.

V. The testing of wood stoves

The importance of testing

The testing of stoves is of vital importance for the following main reasons:

—it permits a better understanding of the processes of combustion and heat recuperation
—it renders it possible to determine the functioning of individual components in stoves, and to isolate weaknesses with a view to improving overall performance
—it assists stove makers with the design and manufacture of sturdier and more efficient models
—it enables designers to assess the reactions of users and adapt their stoves in the light of particular needs and preferences
—it indicates which stove models are unsuitable for further promotion
—it provides other stove makers with valuable information and gives them the basis for a comparison with their own models.

Standard testing procedures should supply all the data necessary to assess and compare, in an objective manner, the technical characteristics of stoves and, in particular, their respective fuel efficiencies.

The ultimate goal of stove makers is to design models which are capable of being understood, properly operated and maintained by the intended beneficiaries. Local acceptance may be greatly enhanced if the users feel that they have participated in the development of 'their' stoves. This involvement should ideally extend to testing and procedures must consequently be kept as simple and effective as possible. No particular qualifications — beyond a sound primary education — should be required or necessary for the performance of basic tests. This is not, of course, to deny the importance of more advanced methodologies for testing, on a sample basis, in the field or in properly staffed and equipped technical laboratories. However, it is essential to preserve a sense of proportion so that both approaches — the simple and the more sophisticated — may complement each other.

In many European countries it is standard practice to subject new stove models to

Figure 84 *Box-shaped hot air generator.*

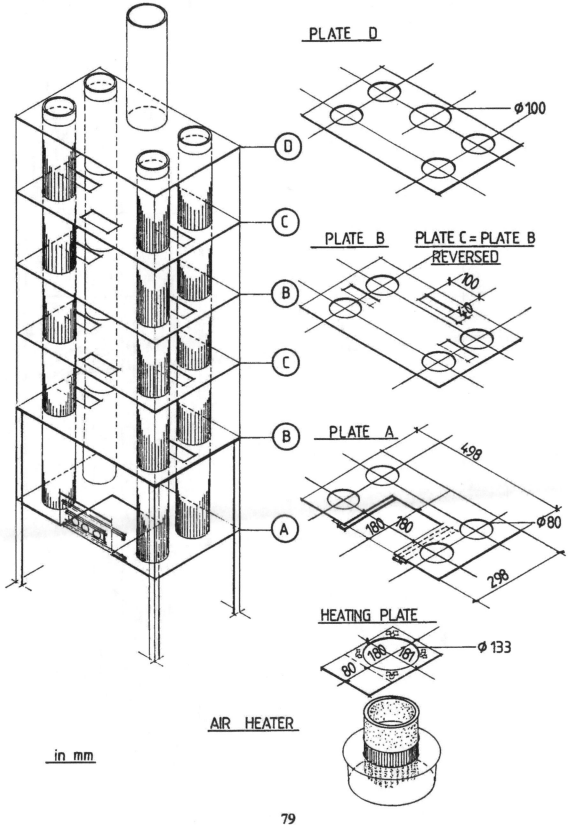

PLATE D

Ø100

PLATE B   PLATE C = PLATE B
                          REVERSED

100

D

C

B

C

B

A

PLATE A

498

180 180   Ø80

298

HEATING PLATE

180 181   Ø 133

80

in mm

AIR HEATER

79

Figure 85 *Flow of air and gases.*

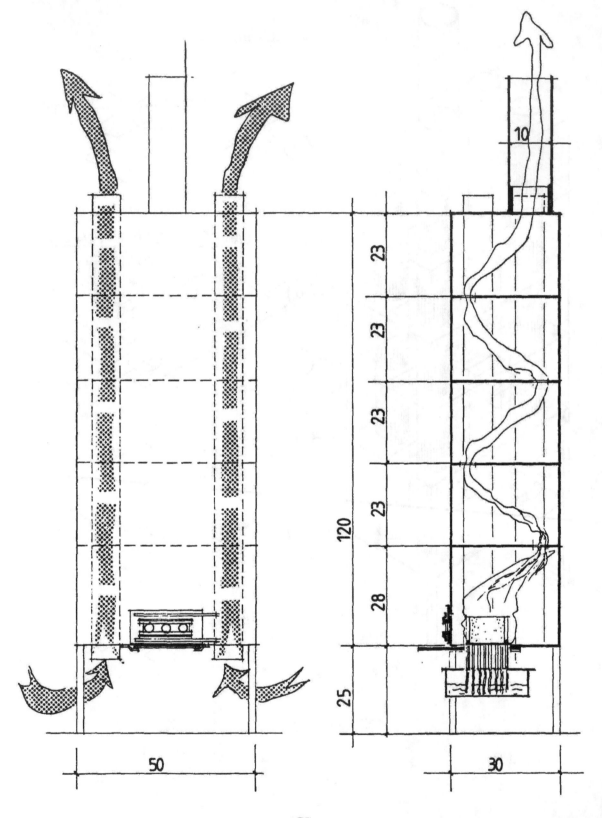

laboratory testing prior to granting permission for their commercial promotion. It is instructive to note that, in almost all cases, the complicated methods used in this screening fully endorse the results it is possible to obtain using simple procedures such as those described below. In addition, such simple methods have probably contributed as much, if not more, to the design of more efficient, simple cookstoves as their more sophisticated counterparts.

The importance of field experience. Before attempting to design and test improved stoves for any given community, it is most important to devote some time to cooking, by traditional means, with the local population in order thoroughly to assimilate existing local customs, needs and preferences. These of course will be of fundamental relevance in assessing the kind of innovations (new cooking methods, pots etc.) the community is likely to accept or resist.

Basic specifications of all cookstoves. Basically, communities all over the world — in developing and developed countries alike — prefer stoves which:
—enable food to be brought rapidly to the boil
—allow heat to be regulated for slow simmering
—consume as little fuel as possible
—provide the maximum of user comfort
—cost little.

To these basic specifications, which must be met in all new designs, should be added particular local requirements which the designer may only effectively determine after having become fully acquainted, through extensive practical experience, with the prevailing cooking procedures and traditions.

Once the designer has established the needs his stoves must fulfil he may turn his attention to the question of obtaining maximum fuel-efficiency. Herein lies the overriding importance of evolving standard testing procedures.

Work on testing standards. In recent years considerable efforts have been expended on trying to draw up universally accepted standards for the testing of wood stoves. There have, notably, been several major international meetings devoted to the problem, including those convened in Louvain (Belgium) in March 1982, Marseilles (France) in May 1982 and Arlington (USA) in December 1982. Such meetings aimed to arrive at standardised procedures which would facilitate the comparison of fuel-efficient stoves destined for developing countries.[29]

The adoption of such norms would represent a major boost to efforts to introduce fuel-efficient stoves, as clearly inefficient models — which should not be promoted, especially in countries suffering from severe shortages of firewood — could be readily identified and discarded early in their development.

The norms constitute an excellent starting point. Naturally, they may be subject to review at regular intervals as work on designing and manufacturing fuel-efficient stoves progresses. Shortcomings may thus be ironed out in the course of time. The important thing at this stage, however, is that there finally exist simple, universally-acceptable testing procedures. The author recommends that these should be adopted and applied by all concerned as soon as possible.

The water boiling tests contained in this booklet conform in essential aspects with the preliminary suggestions made by the group of experts meeting in Arlington, which were still under elaboration at the time of printing.

The tests finally agreed upon are likely to

29. See, *inter alia*, the proceedings of the expert meeting organised by Volunteers in Technical Assistance (VITA) — *Testing the Efficiency of Wood-Burning Cookstoves, Provisional International Standards*, Arlington, Virginia 2209-2079 USA, December 1982.

be fairly detailed so as to avoid ambiguities. In the meantime, simplified versions are presented below in order to facilitate the task of field workers, whose equipment is usually limited to a wristwatch and scales.

The short water boiling test

The water boiling test is generally recognised as a quick, simple means of ascertaining, under field conditions, the performance of several different stoves or, alternatively, that of a single model under varying operating conditions.

The first step is to establish and record the weight, species and dimensions of the air-dried fuel wood (which should, preferably, be cut into pieces with a diameter of about 2 to 3 cm). Similarly it is necessary to record:

—ambient air temperature
—climatic conditions (wind, rain etc.), and whether the test was conducted under shelter or in the open air
—the weight of the pots as well as the initial weight and temperature of the water.

Drawings and descriptions of the stove and pots are also very helpful.

The procedure for the test is as follows:
a) a measured quantity of wood is placed next to the stove.
b) a pot is weighed and filled with water. The quantity of water measured in kilogrammes should correspond to that commonly used by families in everyday cooking (say 4 to 6 litres) and should fill the pot to about ⅔ of its capacity. Whether or not the pot is covered with a lid should be recorded.
c) the fire is lit and the flame maintained in the best possible manner.
d) the time taken to bring the water to a **brisk** boil is recorded.[30]
e) the fire should then be immediately extinguished with sand or earth.
f) charcoal and unburnt wood is removed from the fire, separated and weighed.

g) the weight of unburnt wood ~~and~~ charcoal[31] is then deducted from the initial quantity placed next to the stove in order to arrive at the total amount of wood consumed.
h) finally, the total amount of wood consumed is divided by the number of litres of water boiled to give the **Specific Wood Consumption (SWC)** of the stove.

In the absence of specialised equipment for determining the exact composition of the gases leaving the chimney, a simple statement as to the transparency, or otherwise, of the smoke constitutes a good working guide to the efficiency and correct functioning of the stove.

An examination of the ashes left in the stove, noting in particular their colour and consistency, is also very instructive.

As a basis for comparison it should be noted that, using a well-managed open fire, it is possible to arrive at an SWC coefficient of 0.1 or slightly higher (i.e. 100 g, or slightly more, of wood per litre of water boiled).

Similar results obtained on enclosed stoves may be considered as being just acceptable. However, stoves designed to economise on wood should give a lower SWC reading.

The long water boiling test

This test is commenced with a cold stove in exactly the same manner as the first test. A given quantity of wood (say between 1.0 to 1.5 kg) is placed next to the stove. The time of lighting of the fire is noted and the subsequent procedure is as follows:

30. The author does not recommend keeping the water boiling for 15 minutes as has been suggested by some experts. It is submitted that this procedure adds little to the assessment of a stove's performance and runs contrary to the standard advice given to stove users, who should be encouraged to avoid fast boiling as it brings about unnecessary wastage of fuel.
31. For this calculation, the weight of charcoal remaining in the fire should be multiplied by a coefficient of 1.5 in order to give a figure closer to the calorific value of firewood.

a) the time taken for the water to boil briskly is recorded.

b) the fire is maintained at a level just sufficient to keep the water simmering, the available wood being used as sparingly as possible until it has all been consumed and the water ceases to simmer (i.e. when the temperature drops 5°C below boiling). Efforts should be made to keep the water simmering for as close as possible to one hour after reaching boiling point.

c) at the conclusion of the test the pot and remaining contents are weighed in order to establish the weight of water evaporated.

d) the total weight of wood consumed is measured in the same manner as in the first test (usually very little charcoal is left on the grate).

To simplify and shorten the tests the author suggests another variant, namely to carry out the test in one hour, counting from the time when the stove is lit. This serves to highlight the fact that cooking times in excess of one hour should not be encouraged — especially in countries gravely affected by fuelwood shortages. If boiling and simmering lasts about three-quarters of an hour, one may calculate consumption of wood per litre/hour boiling with a minimum of error.

It may be mentioned here that, on a practical level, it is exceedingly difficult in field conditions to dose the input of firewood to the stove in such a way as to achieve the conclusion of the boiling process in precisely one hour. Indeed, in most fuel-efficient stoves, particularly those made from clay, boiling tends to continue for some time after all the fuel has been consumed. Thus, to interrupt the test after one hour, when the water is still boiling, may produce a misleading indication of the characteristics of the stove. In any case, it would be necessary to present the result of the test after an adjustment to bring the real time of simmering in line with the set time of one hour.

Conclusions. If conducted under the same climatic conditions, using the same quality of firewood, pots and quantities of water — as well as comparable operator skills — the results of both water boiling tests offer stove makers and local populations an excellent indication of the relative characteristics of different stove models.

It is strongly recommended, for basic reference and comparison purposes, always to conduct parallel tests on a well-managed or protected open fire.

For professional stove makers the two tests, if properly and reliably conducted, offer all the information needed to calculate the performance and, particularly, the fuel efficiency of stoves. **Thus, they correspond equally well to simple and more sophisticated requirements.**

Demonstration of the relative fuel efficiency of stoves

The author recommends conducting, at village level, a practical demonstration of the relative efficiency of the stoves used locally.

This demonstration does not furnish any more technical data than the tests described above.

It does, however, provide villagers with an excellent **visual** appreciation of the relative values of each stove tested.

The object of the demonstration is to determine how many litres of water may be brought to the boil on each stove using a given quantity of firewood (eg. 1.0 kg or 1.5 kg).

Procedure for stoves with one opening.
a) the first step is to prepare two identical cooking pots.

b) each pot is filled with an equal volume of water. The quantity used should correspond to about two-thirds of the total capacity of the pot, and represents normal family requirements (i.e. between 4 to 6 litres).

c) the fire is started and the flame maintained in the best possible manner.

d) as soon as its contents are boiling properly, the first pot is removed and replaced with the second.

e) the first pot is then cooled, refilled with cold water and the sequence repeated until all the wood has been consumed.

f) at the end of the demonstration the number of litres boiled is noted together with the temperature of water in the remaining pot.

Procedure for stoves with two openings. The procedure is identical in all respects, except that **three** rather than two pots of cold water are prepared at the outset of the test. Pot A is placed on opening 1 and pot B on opening 2. Pot C is held in reserve. As soon as its contents have been brought to the boil, pot A is removed and pot B (with its partially heated contents) is transferred to opening 1. Pot C is then immediately placed in opening 2 and the sequence continued until the demonstration has been completed.

The demonstration is well understood and usually enjoyed by villagers, especially as it arouses their competitive spirit.

Improving the reliability of tests

The value of tests may be increased if more exact measuring instruments are used (e.g. scales, thermometers, anemometers and hydrometers). Such precision equipment also improves the comparability of a series of tests conducted in different countries and regions under varying climatic conditions. This being said, the tests have the advantage of providing useful data even when carried out carefully by villagers possessing only basic equipment such as a watch, simple scales and measuring jars. These people have no pretensions to making measurements of the accuracy required for international scientific comparison but merely wish to determine, as simply as possible, which stoves offer the best performance whilst meeting the particular requirements of their community.

The hierarchy of tests

The above tests have been arranged according to a hierarchy. It is not necessary to conduct the entire series on every stove. For example, if the short boiling test reveals that a given model is clearly unsatisfactory, there is little point in proceeding to the following test. The stove in question should either be abandoned or redesigned. However, if the stove passes the first hurdle, it may be subjected to the long boiling test in order to assess its suitability, or otherwise, for selective dissemination for the purpose of monitoring its performance under real conditions. The emphasis during such preliminary field testing should be on ascertaining durability, ease of operation, maintenance and repair, user comfort, acceptability and the suitability of the cooking pots and cooking methods to be used in conjunction with the stove. Only after the successful completion of all the above stages should a prototype stove be considered for promotion on a larger scale.

During initial field testing it may be justified occasionally to conduct tests similar to those described in this section, but using given quantities of food rather than water.

The procedure involved, however, is far more laborious and, as there are more variables introduced, less meaningful. In addition, comparisons with tests conducted elsewhere, even on the same type of stove, are extremely difficult (if not virtually impossible) due to differences in types of food, local tastes, cooking methods and so on. (We only have to compare different people's definition of when an egg is boiled or beef is cooked to appreciate this.)

Whilst food boiling tests conducted in the users' households certainly provide useful information on local customs, needs, preferences and the like, it is submitted that they do not add any information

concerning fuel efficiency over and above that which it is possible to obtain, more reliably, by recourse to water boiling tests.

For all tests the author suggests that fuel efficiency should be calculated with respect to **direct** cooking. Heat recovered, for example, on a second opening or by a hot water tank, which is not sufficient to boil or simmer water is **irrelevant as far as direct cooking is concerned** and should **not** be incorporated into calculations of SWC. Even more irrelevant in this respect is, of course, heat radiated by the stove.

At all times it is important to remember that, when working amongst poor communities, the overriding aim of the stove designer must be to achieve maximum fuelwood economies.

Reporting forms

It is essential to record all readings taken during cooking tests in an orderly fashion on standardised reporting forms. However, in drawing up such forms, due allowance must be made for the educational level of the field workers directly involved. As has been stated above, such people should possess a solid primary education but surely cannot be expected to cope with advanced statistical concepts. Notions such as standard deviation, coefficient of variation, standard error etc. are useful to persons possessing the academic qualifications needed to comprehend and interpret them. However, they may be beyond the grasp of field workers, who would thus be unable to co-operate. The adoption of over-complex forms could also lead to the creation of small groups of 'professional' stove testers indulging in the preparation of sophisticated reports which are not always understood by those in the field. The solution would seem to be to introduce testing on two levels. The first level would involve simple procedures and forms conceived for those actually building and using stoves in the field. The second would be the province of academics suitably qualified to conduct more complex

tests, on a sample basis — prefera[bly in] properly equipped laboratories. It s[hould] be stressed, however, that sophisti[cated] testing involves considerable expend[iture] and may drain a disproportionate am[ount] of funds from the modest resou[rces] currently available for the act[ual] development and promotion of effici[ent] wood-burning stoves.

Other tests on wood stoves

When working on simple, yet efficien[t] stoves destined for developing countries the designer is well advised to maintai[n] close contact with specialised firms manufacturing wood stoves in industrialised countries — particularly those located in Europe or the United States.

Indeed, we are currently experiencing a revival of interest in wood stoves in economically developed countries, and manufacturers are constantly striving to improve specifications and produce new designs to meet a wide variety of consumer needs.

Such firms measure the performance of the stoves they produce in **quantitative** terms and inform their customers accordingly. Their measurements are based on norms imposed by the relevant government authorities — which are also responsible for checking that the claims made by the manufacturers are in conformity with the established procedures.

Hopefully in the future, the designers of stoves destined for developing countries will be able to agree on similar uniform norms for the quantitative measurement of performance. Ultimately, the basic norms should be identical for rich and poor countries alike — especially as the differences with respect to materials and technical characteristics will tend to diminish with time. In the meantime, however, there exist in Europe and the United States a number of laboratories specialising in the testing of wood burning

stoves. Designers of simple stoves may occasionally commission these to conduct a thorough examination and critical analysis of their models.

The Eindhoven formula

Aware of the work being undertaken on the testing of wood stoves, and in pursuit of at least some degree of scientific exactness, specialists from the Eindhoven and Apeldoorn Polytechnic Schools in the Netherlands have expanded on the water boiling test by suggesting a simple formula for measuring the degree of fuel efficiency of stoves. This formula, which is relatively easy to apply in the field and which has been used to test all the models featured in this book, is given in Table 2.

The Eindhoven formula provides an indication of the performance of any given stove and emphasises the importance of a **cooking system** which, apart from stoves and fuels, also includes cooking pots. It also constitutes a first step towards introducing a much-needed quantitative measurement of stove performance.

Table 2. The Eindhoven formula

$$\eta = \frac{m_w.C(t_b - t_i) + m_v.R}{m_f.B}$$

where:

η	=	fuel-efficiency rate	
m_w	=	initial amount of water in the pan	(kg)
m_v	=	amount of water evaporated during experiment	(kg)
m_f	=	amount of fuel burnt	(kg)
C	=	specific heat of water	(kJ/kg. K)
t_b	=	temperature of water	(°C)
t_i	=	initial temperature of water in pan	(°C)
R	=	heat of evaporation of water at atmospheric pressure and 100°C	(kJ/kg)
B	=	combustion value of wood used	(kJ/kg)

Values for the various quantities used were:

C = 4.2 kJ/kg.K

R = 2256.9 kJ/kg

B = 19,883 kJ/kg

86

This being said, when interpreting the stove efficiency figures obtained using the formula, it is important to make suitable allowance for **variable factors**, such as climatic conditions, the shape and design of the pots, the heat value of the wood and the skill of the stove operator — all of which may influence the results considerably.

Provided, however, that the tests are conducted under similar conditions, the formula offers a very good means of comparing the fuel efficiency of different models.

It is submitted that no significant improvements in stove design and construction may be achieved without some such quantitative measuring of performance. The Eindhoven formula goes a long way towards answering this need and has served the author and his collaborators well in their research.

However, in order to avoid possible mis-interpretation, the results obtained using the formula should be accompanied by data recorded during water boiling tests. This has been the procedure adopted throughout this book.